For Rin,
Max and
Ari

When
Life
Is Not
Peachy

*Real–life lessons
in recovery from
heartache, loss
& tough times*

Pip Lincolne

murdoch books
Sydney | London

Contents

Introduction 7

HELLO

Introduction

If life has taken a difficult turn, chances are you are not feeling very much like yourself.

MAYBE IT HAS TAKEN YOU some time to get to this unfamiliar place, or perhaps it's been sudden. Either way, you may be experiencing lots of awful feelings and wondering what the heck you're meant to do now.

This book is here to help.

Tough times dotted my life for a number of years, and there were moments I honestly wondered if I'd ever recover.

But as I looked at the people around me, I could see many of them were also dealing with their own painful challenges: the loss of much-loved family members or friends, serious illnesses, traumatic relationships, overwhelming or unexpected life changes.

Not only did they speak of feeling isolated in their sadness, and unsure of how to deal with their own big feelings, they noted that others didn't really know how to help them either.

When I was struggling through my own hard times, I started to write down the things that helped me, the things that were hard, things the experts said might prove a healing salve ... and slowly but surely, a book took shape.

I wanted to put my heart on my sleeve and talk about some of the difficult times and feelings many of us battle through, just in case it might help other people going through hard times.

Oh my gosh
it has been
a lot. A lot
to deal with.

That said, I didn't really want to focus too much on how I got to a sad place. This is not a memoir, as my psychologist has pointed out to me.

Let's just say the last few years included several deaths in the family, deaths of beloved pets, challenging mental and physical ill health and the breakdown of a difficult 23-year relationship. Oh my gosh it has been a lot. A lot to deal with. A lot of suffering. A lot of feelings.

I thought finding some common ground in the feelings that these sorts of tough times spark might be helpful to others, and potentially a way to find my own way out of the fog.

Of course, everyone's circumstances are different, and our responses are different too — but there are also lots of ways we are similar when tough times strike.

I wanted to talk a bit more about those similarities, and how we might band together to navigate really hard days, weeks and months. Because if we can't share the most fragile and human bits of ourselves — to bolster and support each other — then what are we even doing?!

I thought finding some common ground in the feelings that these sorts of tough times spark might be helpful to others.

Please note that this book is not an expert guide, and by no means a substitute for specific and professional help — although it does contain lots of bits and bobs from actual experts, too, and some resources you might find helpful. Rather, it's a guide from someone who has lived through some hard things and made it out the other side in one piece — and actually feeling a little stronger and wiser as a result.

If you have endured loss, difficulty, trauma or other sad events, then I hope this book might help you snaffle some more peaceful moments and take the edge off your suffering — even just for a wee while.

Sending
squeezes
to you,
Pip

CHAPTER 1

Help me, my heart is broken

If you are reading this, you are probably already heartbroken.

Bloody hell.

I AM SO sorry this is happening to you. I am so sorry things have gone so wrong.

Perhaps you are sitting quietly, trying to process these sentences, and indeed where you are at in your life.

Intermittently shaking your head in disbelief, unsure how this could even have happened, how you could have found yourself feeling so at sea. Possibly clinging onto the doona/large glass of wine/comfort kebab/or yourself for dear freaking life.

Perhaps you are nursing an actual *physical* pain in your heart (and other places) and thinking, *Why does it feel like this? Aargh, help! When will it end?* Please accept this from-afar hug, through the pages of this book.

Know that I am thinking *Eff this, you don't deserve this shit*. I truly am. I'm in your corner. I have navigated the awfulness of my own version of where you are.

When something terrible has happened, the physical ache in the heart is more than just an expression snaffled from a '60s love song. It's an *actual*, painful emotional *and* physical condition.

Heartache in the wake of loss is a very real and deep sort of pain. It's surprising and scary. Breathtakingly stabby and overwhelming and frankly every bit as horrifying as the creepy things you imagined lurking under the bed when you were a kid.

The early days and weeks (sometimes months or more) of broken-heartedness appear to be entirely made up of injured body parts, lost selves, disappearing hopes and dreams, and much-wanted things that now feel utterly impossible or unattainable.

This ache is a two-fold trauma. Not only are you trying to process all kinds of confusing thoughts and emotions inside your brain, but there's a weighty, pressing — at times unbearable, at other times quietly tick-tocking — pushing ache in your chest as well.

Perhaps it's not just your chest? It might extend through your upper body and into your battle-weary and exhausted head, too. Or your ears even? The back of your stinging throat? Perhaps it's your eyes as well, blurry from tears and swirling words.

This kind of hurt is so hard to bear — and when you are feeling this way it seems you will never feel *any other* way.

But you will. I promise. I truly do.

So why does it hurt like this?

Why does the sadness and shock wash over us and seep so very, very deeply inwards?

Perhaps it's because some very primal parts of us are awakened when we're going through big and difficult stuff. Our 'fight or flight' response activates, flooding our brain with stress hormones, and our muscles tense up madly in response.

Suddenly, you might have a cracking headache, a stiff neck, and a chest that feels like a giant angry bear is giving it an actual bear hug or sitting its giant bear bum on you, your body completely concealed by its hefty and heavy frame. It feels horrendous.

These bewildering physical feelings may give rise to panic and anxiety, which cause a whole other kind of fizzy rush and a cracking ache that adds an unwelcome dose of terror to the pain.

This is not fair. Let's be clear on that. But please understand …

a)
there are good reasons for these bad feelings

b)
you can't help feeling this way

c)
these feelings are normal

d)
you're going to be okay.

Knowledge is power, they say. So let's push on.

Just when we think we've suffered enough, our worried bodies, in a bid to protect us, become a strange new land.

As your panicked, weirdly firmed-up muscles commandeer as many resources from your body as possible in a bid to keep you safe, other bits of you start to suffer in response.

In this 'robbing Peter to pay Paul' scenario, you might end up with a stomach ache (as blood is diverted away from important digestive work), and your immunity might dip (making you vulnerable to viruses and other nasties). This is why people so very often get sick after they've suffered an emotional blow.

Stress hormones might continue to wreak havoc, disturbing your sleep patterns, interfering with your appetite and generally making you feel strung out, and out of sorts.

The bad news? Apparently, you *are* strung out. Science tells us that the emotional toll of heartbreak turns on areas in your brain that also contribute to addiction or cravings.

This might be why dealing with a loss feels like a kind of withdrawal, complete with painful physical and emotional symptoms.

The good news is ...

It won't always feel this way. One day you will feel way less terrible. So hold on to that thought and let's talk about what to do in the meantime to help ease the pain a little.

PERHAPS YOU MIGHT BE DEALING WITH:

- unfamiliar scary emotions
- a worrying numbness
- deep sadness
- lots of crying
- guilt
- feelings of hopelessness
- anger, fear, hypervigilance, panic, apathy, irritability, confusion — argh!
- difficulty concentrating
- intrusive thoughts
- memory problems
- social anxiety or self-isolation
- constant rumination
- weird breathing — too much or not enough
- disinterest in things you usually like
- loss of appetite or increase in appetite
- flashbacks and awful memories
- nightmares
- feeling threatened
- varied physical aches, pains and chronic health conditions
- digestive issues
- issues with reproductive bits, such as period problems
- sleeplessness or sleeping more than usual
- misuse of alcohol and/ or drugs
- many other things that are unique to you, dear reader

The feelings above are normal responses to a terrible time, but sometimes these feelings are relentless and may get in the way of daily life. This can spark the sort of anxiety and depression which needs treatment.

If this happens to you, know that you are in good company (i.e. me), and that I have managed to clunkily work through it — and with the benefit of hindsight I have some good ideas on what might help you. (Including calling in the experts if need be — but more on that later.)

How to cope in the raw, early days

You've probably heard the expression, 'The only way out is through'? Well, turns out it's true.

Thankfully, there are a whole heap of ways you can look after yourself as your heart and head adapt to this unsettling and unexpected new life. I'll go into lots more of those as we settle into this book, but let's start with some immediate first aid for the urgent physical and emotional pain that's darkening your doorstep.

Let's do a quick little triage, right this minute.

Take some over-the-counter painkillers

When the physical pain of my beleaguered heart got too much, taking some paracetamol (also known as acetaminophen) really did help. This might sound like poppycock, but take it from me, it truly can provide some temporary relief when you're feeling like a piece of smashed-up poop.

It seems that this easing of emotional upset isn't down to a placebo effect. Studies have found that acetaminophen (a.k.a. paracetamol) can dull the intensity of emotions, and take the edge off physical pain. So if you're feeling overwhelmed by all the terrible feelings and are navigating a whopping dose of heartache, you might like to try taking some paracetamol as your first port of pain-relieving call.

Let's do
a quick
little triage,
right this
minute.

Obviously, *always* follow the directions and observe the health warnings and contraindications on the packet, because we don't want you all jacked-up on these entry-level painkillers.

Try to get some sleep

For some of us, falling into a quicksand-resembling slumber is the logical response to being hurt. Everything feels heavy, cloudy and resistant, and staying alert seems impossible as our bodies battle to make sense of what's happening and try to best respond.

For others, sleepless nights — or, at the very least, highly interrupted sleep cycles — lie ahead. Falling asleep at 6 pm on the way home from work. Waking up in some far-flung part of the city, pressed up against the bus window. Feeling super-alert until 2 am. Passing out. Waking up at 4 am wired and worn out. Watching *Real Housewives* until the sun comes up. Just me? But you get the picture.

Sleep is vital for good emotional and physical health, and it's especially important when we're recovering from a trauma.

Not only does deep sleep provide a reprieve from difficult times, it helps us to manage and regulate our emotional responses to tricky situations.

It's easy to stress out about lack of sleep, but let's not do that. Let's know that we're doing our best, trying to do stuff that will encourage more snoozing, and that one day it will be better than this.

But how to sleep when the situation you are in is replaying various scenarios over and over in your head? Or you are suffering the physical embodiments of anxiety (hello racing heart!)?

We're going to look at sleep strategies in a lot more detail in Chapter 5, but because it's so vital, we're going to do a quick crash course here as well as part of our emergency triage.

IF YOUR SLEEP CYCLE IS ALL MESSED UP, IT MIGHT BE HELPFUL TO *AVOID* THE FOLLOWING:

- sleeping next to charging devices like your phone or laptop — they emit light, which some people think disturbs sleep
- falling asleep watching TV shows or movies
- having too much light in your bedroom
- drinking caffeine in the late afternoon
- drinking alcohol, which interferes with deep sleep
- being too hot or too cold
- having an erratic routine, because this throws out your body's natural circadian rhythm, which regulates sleep and wakefulness
- eating too much or not enough
- doing zero exercise

I'm not going to tell you *not* to do the things above, because gosh knows you've suffered enough. I'm just going to whisper them and move on. You do what you're able to do, when you're able to do it. Do what makes you feel a bit more okay.

My own sleep patterns did eventually right themselves once I learned to put sleep first and stopped worrying about waking up super-early and being productive (which is what I used to love to do).

Instead, I let myself sleep in for an hour longer each day, and made sure I did the kind of afternoon and evening things that would help me sleep more solidly.

**THINGS THAT HELPED ME FEEL CALM ENOUGH
TO DOZE OFF AT BEDTIME INCLUDED:**

- having a nourishing dinner, and making sure I'd eaten enough during the day
- not having bracing cups of tea or coffee after lunch time
- doing 10 minutes of gentle yoga before bed
- listening to a chapter of an audio book
- hugging a hot water bottle
- having a hot bath with a few drops of lavender or eucalyptus oil in it before bed
- reading a snippet from *The Pocket Pema Chödrön*

Don't get me wrong, there were times I still watched at least two episodes (possibly four) of something on Netflix before I went to sleep because I'm obviously a reckless rule-breaker.

Stretch, breathe, just keep moving

I have never been hugely into yoga — but I know *now* that I would have felt a lot better if I'd moved my body a bit more during those darkest days. And because I *didn't* move very much, preferring to lie in the foetal position under the blankets and binge every season of *Gossip Girl* in just a few days, I made myself feel *much* stiffer, creakier and generally even *more* broken than ever.

The brokenness was in my knees and elbows and neck and back and hips. It was like someone had over-turned a key, winding up all my moving parts until the springs broke and everything grated and crunched and made a truly ugly sound.

I was so stiff, in fact, that sometimes, because I could hardly turn my neck, I could only drive in a straight line. If I had to dogleg left or right, I had to turn my whole torso like a kind of robot lady.

I am guessing this stiffness was partly an extension of those 'fight or flight' side-effects we mentioned earlier. Those muscles that get oversupplied with escape-enhancing surges of blood end up utterly fatigued and simply seize up.

Had I been gently moving my body as I pushed on through into my new life, I probably wouldn't have been the physical embodiment of 'stuck'.

It was only a year later, after battling some health issues that required a more disciplined response to caring for myself, that I started doing some basic yoga and began to feel better.

The first three times I did yoga, I actually cried with a gushing sort of physical and emotional relief. It felt like an unwinding was beginning, and what started as a squeaky trickle became a kind of cleansing torrent.

Thankfully I was at home and not sobbing my way through a hot yoga class with someone's buttocks in my face. I was amidst the shag-pile and the coffee table and a pile of *National Geographic* magazines in my living room. The only witnesses to this teary tide during my YouTube yoga classes were some brass ducks on my window ledge and an elephant with its trunk up.

Of course, your body might be fairly brimming with vim and vigour as you thrash your way out of your own heartbroken days. But if your physical body is feeling 'stuck' like mine was, a bit Tin Man pre-oil can, then maybe my story will reassure you that things *do* shift and that you *will* begin to feel better, in time.

*SPOILER ALERT
There's a lot of crying
(and anger, and anxiety)
in this book, but I turned out
okay in the end, so don't worry.
I share the tears so that if it's *you*
sobbing into your yoga mat,
you will feel less alone.

Find a person who needs your help

Everyone deals with heartbreak differently. Some of us go to ground (like me), while others need to dive into a pond of favourite people and let them gather us up.

But all of us can benefit from shifting the focus off ourselves and tapping into someone else's needs for a while.

What kind of someone else? It could be a friend who needs a hand/some help painting their front fence/a nice casserole. It could be someone at work who is struggling in a particular area. The old lady down the road, the person who can't reach the box of cereal at the supermarket, or the Facebook acquaintance who let on they are desperate for that unused slow cooker/baby carrier/cobwebby fire pit stored under your house.

Reaching out to provide practical help to others, and in fact simply being kind to others, gives us a hit of the feel-good hormones that help take the sharp edges off life, even if just for a short while.

Keep in mind that supporting someone else *emotionally* should probably not be on your to-do list right now. Not only do you have a lot on your plate, but you may find that the negative experiences of others may even heighten your own anxiety or deepen your low mood. Instead of counselling your stressed-out friend, send them a message to let them know you are thinking about them.

Let your pal know you love them, but remember the priority is really to make your days a care package for *yourself*, and to attend to your own emotional and physical recovery.

Put your own oxygen mask on first, as they say in the classics.

Have a hot bath

Water is a great unraveller, and a hot bath provides not only a muscle-relaxing salve but also an excellent place to cry. (Not even kidding, sometimes I get in the bath with a book about a woman battling with nature — hawks or bears or avalanches or whatever — and I just end up having a very cathartic sob into the suds.)

A hot bath, with a few drops of something that encourages you to breathe deeply and restore a bit of balance to your body, can offer some speedy first aid for lacklustre souls.

A hot bath will also help you sleep better, as your body heats up and then cools down when you hop out. The cooling-down bit makes you feel sleepy.

Indeed, recent research has suggested that warming yourself up in a long hot bath can have some of the same benefits as exercise. This makes it perfect for people who are feeling under the weather, with benefits including lowering blood pressure and better regulating blood sugar.

Perhaps you don't have a bath at your house? Maybe you could pop over and borrow your mum's or best friend's bath? If not, there are other hot things that help, too. Like these:

hot shower	hot water bottle	hot tea	hot toddy	hot chips!

There's much more on bathing in Chapter 9 — but I just wanted to slip in a brief mention here of its many benefits so that you get yourself in the bath or under a hot shower ASAP.

Remember: this, too, will pass

The other thing I'd really like to impart here is that what you are going through is temporary.

As permanently life-changing as your crisis may be, your response to it is not permanent.

You will not always feel terrible. You may continue to view what has happened as terrible, but you *will* get some respite from these feelings eventually.

It can be truly impossible to imagine that things will ever be okay again, and I understand that, because I have been there.

DIAL FOR HELP

If you need extra support right now or someone to talk to, the following mental health lines can help.

- Australia (Lifeline): 13 11 14
- New Zealand (Lifeline): 0800 543 354
- United Kingdom: 08457 909 090
- United States: 1800 273 8255

- Canada: 1866 277 3553 (outside Montreal); 514 723 4000 (Montreal)

> I promise you that even the worst feelings in the universe do change or pass ...

While there were times I felt it would be so much easier to just disappear, something in me still clung to the hope that someday I might *not* feel this way. Thankfully I am now on the mend, with some help from a GP and psychologist and some trusty medication.

I promise you that even the worst feelings in the universe do change or pass ... and that everyone has somebody who is so very glad that they are around.

Matt Haig wrote a brilliant book about navigating a serious mental health crisis, called *Reasons To Stay Alive*. Matt woke up one day with severe depression and found himself struggling with thoughts about ending his own life. In his book he discusses what he went through very openly, in the hope that it can make others feel less isolated in their own experience.

Matt notes that depression is very common, and does not discriminate, and he very wisely reasons that mental ill health should be treated as compassionately and practically as any other illness, pointing out that many of the most brilliant people on the planet have gone through dark periods in their lives. 'You are no less or more of a man or a woman or a human for having depression than you would be for having cancer or cardiovascular disease or a car accident,' he writes.

Though it might seem like these dark feelings are a sign that you've transformed into a broken sort of person, that's simply not the case. These feelings, as hard as they may be to live with — are temporary in nature, and they *do* pass.

With the right support and/or treatment, things can feel a little better, or even a lot better.

In *Reasons To Stay Alive*, Matt explains that depression is smaller than you, even when it feels vast: 'It operates within you, you do not operate within it. It may be a dark cloud passing across the sky but — if that is the metaphor — you are the sky. You were there before it. And the cloud can't exist without the sky, but the sky can exist without the cloud.'

When I look back at how I was feeling when I was at my worst, I realise that those memories now feel fuzzy, and the depth of my past sadness is very hard to reconnect to. I can focus more on the sky that Matt talks about, rather than the clouds. And even when the clouds drift into view, they look interesting and moody, rather than menacing and looming.

Perhaps that's a sort of protective measure? Perhaps my brain would like me to not revisit just how hard things were.

Even writing about those days makes me feel like a warning system is going off inside me, saying: 'Don't look back. It's upwards from here. Keep moving forward. Things are different now. You're okay.'

I know that okay moments will begin to shuffle into your life as the weeks and months pass, too.

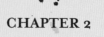

CHAPTER 2

There's a lot of feelings

> 'You can't
> control
> the places
> mental health
> takes you.'
>
> •
>
> Rosie
> Waterland

Feeling lost

Right now, every single thing in your life might seem pointless or wrong. You might start questioning every little thing you do.

This lost feeling might simply be the overwhelm from losing what anchored you in your life.

I really did feel like my life was winding down. I could not see that I'd ever feel okay again, and mostly wanted to retreat from everything. Circumstances had dulled the world's sparkle for me. Where I'd previously trusted in the magic of life, now I felt silly and ripped-off, realising that all the best efforts can't actually determine how everything will impact our life. Sometimes we get what we least deserve, and we just have to respond to this as best we can.

It shakes your faith to know that striving to be as good as you can may not make good things happen — and indeed the shit can hit the fan without warning and render you the saddest and most disappointed sack in the history of sad, disappointed sacks.

But you don't need to change it all up right now.

Give it a few months. Talk to your friends and family. Discuss the bits of your life you're most concerned about, and then listen to yourself, to your heart of hearts — because usually, at the core of things, we know what's right for us. So create some space and have a good, deep 'pros and cons' think about where to next, and why.

Feeling isolated

Ugh. Everyone else is having a good time and living life as though yours has not fallen apart. How bloody dare they? The world is spinning merrily in your joyless absence, and you are feeling on the outside of everyone else's amplified happiness.

When your heart is like shattered honeycomb, most things people do on social media or out there in the wider world will splinter it a tiny bit more.

It's not their fault. Maybe it's a bit like childbirth — you can't imagine or remember the pain until you're in it.

Other people's joyous living-of-their-life ignores your fragility, and they really should *stop*, right? Okay, no, not really, but this is a totally normal way of feeling.

You might even be scoffing at other people's perceived woes: 'Wahhh, someone cut me off on the way to Aldi!' or 'Wahhh, I am angry about these pants!'

That's normal, too.

Have a lie down or go for a walk, or look at yourself in the mirror and say, 'One day I will make them pay!' (JOKE.) Or just silently scream, 'Do not invite me to your Erotic Tantric Massage event, Facebook friend. I am having a broken-heart situation!'

Or, simply look at yourself in the mirror and say, 'People can't help if they don't know what's going on.' After all, that's closer to the truth.

Feeling joyless

I think I probably didn't laugh for about ten months. I'm intense like that, I know.

I did do some sort of hysterical gulping at one point, I think. But this was more frightening mania than joy.

I might have sniggered a few times, too, but this was more of a cynical confirmation that the world will never be the same again, rather than a joyful outburst.

But slowly and surely, the laughs returned.

I noticed them sneaking through one day when I was watching *The Real Housewives of New York City*. I figured it was a freak incident. Turns out it wasn't a freak thing at all, but rather some kind of turning of the tide. It was my psyche saying, 'Look, that is quite enough now, let a giggle in now and again, you idiot.'

After the New York *Housewives* it was the Dallas *Housewives*.

Then I started reading a Caitlin Moran book …

And before I realised it, I was actually laughing from the heart — full joy.

Granted, I didn't laugh at an actual thing in my life at the time.

Granted, I caught myself laughing and eyed myself with suspicion and worry.

But also, a little bit of the old me was seeping back in — in 'new' me style.

A few months later I watched *Isn't It Romantic* and I laughed so many times I scared my dog.

Then I watched Ricky Gervais in *After Life* and I laughed and gasped at the same time. (Because seriously, how awful and also kind is he in that series?)

Next, I watched Russell Brand make a shortbread tribute to his wife's vagina on *The Great British Bake Off* and I giggled uncontrollably.

I realised that I was slowly building up my 'joy muscle' again. Which sounds dirty but I'm talking about my *brain*.

Jokes aside, perhaps you are finding yourself in a bit of a joyless place, too? I totally get it. Everyone is different, and I am not sure exactly what will make you feel better, but I will say this: it's a good idea to watch something funny or silly as you start to emerge from the earliest awful days.

It's a good idea to remind yourself that you are allowed to feel a little splodge of happiness or enjoyment in the midst of your struggle. Nobody is grading you on your response to difficulty, trauma, loss or disappointment. Do not grade yourself.

Take these moments when you can because your good self, your brain and your body all need to remember what a little bit of silliness-sparked happiness feels like. Get those happy hormones flowing when you can, even if it's just for a few random moments.

Again, start small.

Heart pain, grief and other physical pain

Tough times make us feel terrible in all kinds of ways, and we're often more susceptible to viruses and infections as our immune system takes a dip.

Getting sick seems miserable in the midst of a crisis or big life change, but when you feel better, you sometimes even *prefer* the pain of being sick to the pain of being heartbroken. At least there is something tangible and finite about the good old flu.

I'm guessing we all know the emotional pain of heartbreak, but we're only just starting to talk more openly about the very real physical pains associated with hard times.

Indeed, research has shown that the hard-working part of the brain that deals with physical pain (the anterior cingulate cortex) also processes emotional pain.

It's brilliant that we're talking more about how physical and emotional pain intersect, because the pain we humans suffer when something has gone wrong truly is not all in our heads.

Cardiologists have documented how patients who have undergone an emotionally stressful experience complain of heart pain, or heart palpitations. And bereavement experts point out that for many of us, grieving seems to involve a huge physical effort, and it is common to feel a bewildering array of symptoms such as tiredness, sleeplessness, headaches and feeling generally unwell, as well as shifts in our appetite and menstrual cycle.

So if you are feeling like the total pox physically, know that it's a perfectly natural response to what you are going through.

In her book *Can You Die of a Broken Heart?*, heart surgeon Dr Nikki Stamp writes about the pain of heartbreak, explaining at length how the physical and the emotional are entwined, and how the mind and heart are truly connected.

'While your body is trying to be helpful,' she writes, 'by setting off a cascade of hormones and nervous system responses to be ready to fight for your survival, these effects can actually hurt your heart when they hang around for too long.'

When seeking
advice, look for
suitably qualified
experts. In other
words, avoid
'blessed' Instagram
gurus and snake-oil
salespeople!

Dr Stamp notes that her own tough time —
navigating a divorce — took its toll on her in
all kinds of ways: 'My clothes hung off me and
my hair was lank. My body was undernourished
and running on adrenaline. My heart hurt so
badly that it was destroying the rest of me in
the process.'

Dr Stamp says properly looking after
ourselves is *key* to getting better, and she
particularly points to the importance of
nourishing food and exercise. She's also an
advocate for practices like mindfulness and
yoga to help our bodies feel their best under
stressful conditions.

Obviously, Dr Stamp is not only a very
clever medical professional, but also a human
who has navigated difficult things. This is a
combination that makes me prick up my ears
when she shares this sort of advice — so please
do that, too. And when seeking advice, look for
experts who are similarly qualified on a number
of fronts. (In other words, avoid 'blessed'
Instagram gurus and snake-oil salespeople!)

If you've lost someone, had a challenging
shock, suffered something terrible, been
exposed to long-term sad or awful times, some
of the bodily symptoms in the box opposite
might be familiar to you.

PHYSICAL SYMPTOMS
ASSOCIATED WITH HARD TIMES

- Fatigue
- Heart pain
- Heart palpitations
- Back ache
- Neck pain
- Limb pain
- Breathing problems
- Sore stomach
- Digestive issues
- Bowel problems
- Headaches
- Joint pain

- Sweating
- Appetite changes
- Menstrual cycle changes
- High blood pressure
- Low iron
- Asthma
- Dizziness
- Nausea
- Shaking
- Weight gain
- Weight loss

Jesus wept. Look at all those things. And there are more. So again, know that if you are feeling like you have been trodden underfoot by a woolly mammoth, this physical and emotional feeling is a real thing that people experience when they are going through a rough time. It's entirely natural, and not your fault.

Of course, this list doesn't even begin to address the physical implications of some of our coping mechanisms at times like this. Drinking too much, smoking, taking drugs, not sleeping, not being able to exercise, eating too much or not enough are ways we might grapple with our lives when things feel crap, and of course they all impact our health.

By noting down your own particular symptoms, you can head to your GP to discuss them further. Be sure to let them know that …

a)
you feel terrible

b)
you are *also* going through a tonne of crapola!

This is the very best way to get to the bottom of your symptoms *and* get the right help for them.

Please don't be afraid to do this. Don't be afraid to cry or unravel, because you'll be in the very best place to get sorted. Plus your GP will always have *tissues* to mop up your tears, *and* non-judgmental ideas on what you can do to feel a little better.

If you feel like you can hardly put your feelings into words — let alone say them out loud to a doctor — turn to Chapter 10 for some tips on that.

In her book, my favourite heart surgeon, Dr Nikki Stamp, points out that the following symptoms *really do* need further investigation from a medical professional:

chest pain

breathlessness

unusual swelling

heart palpitations

worries about your heart health

Like I said, if you won't listen to me, then listen to Dr Stamp!

Honestly, if you are suffering any of the physical woes from the long list on page 35, why not get them checked out and get yourself on the road to feeling better?

And look, even if your physical health is fairly good, it's comforting to find out for sure, right? Nothing. To. Lose.

Please look after your very precious self.

Dealing with hard times requires Olympic-level effort

If other people knew the epic effort required just to get through our heart-stricken days, they would put us on a podium and shower us with confetti and bottles of Champagne and shake our hands and sing the national anthem.

How do hard times make our bodies feel?

Damp

Is there a threshold you have to pass? A time when you have shed the appropriate amount of tears, and you are allowed to live your life with days not strung together by random bursts of sobbing or long weeps? It certainly seems so. While the actual metric volume of tears is hard to pin down, what is true for most is that the tears will hang on far longer than you'd like, and regularly take you by surprise.

Weird things will upset you. Once, I was writing an article about Jamie Oliver, and as I scrolled through Jools Oliver's Instagram account looking for the perfect image to illustrate the piece, my throat caught, my heart panged and suddenly tears rolled down my cheeks. There was something about all those cute and loved-up family photos that made me feel like my own world was further from cute and loved-up than I could bear. Grief suddenly brought up all these notions of what once was, and what I felt I had lost.

Anyway, my point is *damp*. Because *lots* of tears, cold sweats, hot baths, etc.

Constantly heavy

Eyes won't open, lungs won't breathe, veins feel fizzy, heart pounds and flutters, head is heavy, hair feels like an ugly hat, tongue feels too big for mouth, shoulders feel ill-equipped to carry arms, feet feel flat.

Some days, our bodies and minds seem determined to remind us of this mess we're in.

Some days, I'd find myself breathing in and slowly relaxing my overwrought brain. A kind of test — like poking at a bruise — to see if the sad feelings would flood back.

Sometimes they did, and I caught my breath with the sharpness of it all.

But sometimes they didn't and I'd think, perhaps I'm on the mend ...

Scary, on edge and cold

Okay. This is a weird thing, and I am not sure if it happens to everyone ... but every single day, for a long time, I felt cold and the opposite of grounded. I felt like a helium balloon must feel soaring above the clouds.

| And every day I wanted to ... | a) wear too many cardigans | b) have too many blankets on my bed | c) have a bath! |

Mostly I wanted things to curl themselves around me and make me warm, because I was feeling floaty and empty and a bit numb a lot of the time.

I looked it up, and guess what? It's a very common feeling in people who are sad or lonely or depressed. It's just part of feeling crap and getting over hard times.

Feeling ashamed

Sometimes when people go through tough times, they battle that incredibly loaded and seeming all-encompassing feeling known as shame.

Again, this is a weird thing, and I am not sure if it happens to everyone, but if you have managed to shuffle this far without shame knocking on your door, that is brilliant.

For me, shame weighed me down incredibly. I can't fully explain it, but at times I felt like I was living and breathing it. Or that when I started to push on, it was there — ready to trip me up. It would tap me on the shoulder, swivel me around and knock the wind out of me. And I'm not gonna lie, it still happens.

I guess I felt my sense of shame was some sort of strange penance — for what, I have no idea ... something to do with karma, maybe? Not being perfect enough?

But then I heard psychotherapist Dr Joseph Burgo talk about shame during one of my favourite podcasts, *All In The Mind*, and I started to feel a bit better about these complicated feelings that so many of us endure after a crisis.

Dr Burgo says shame is an inevitable part of life. He sees shame as a 'family' of emotions that all share a painful awareness of self. When we feel an emotion in the shame family, he says, our self comes into focus in a way that feels bad. And while feelings like anger or sadness hurt too, there is something about the focus on *ourselves* that makes shame feelings particularly excruciating.

That really struck me, because I was convinced my feelings of shame meant that I was somehow defective, that I was responsible for every difficult thing that ever happened in my life, and that I was a total shambles of a human.

But actually, shame is not a signal that you are a loser or are not coping with life. It's a natural sign that your positive feelings have been stripped away. Learning to accept those 'shameful' feelings as part of the spectrum of emotions is really helpful, because it stops us being quite so hard on ourselves, and can be a catalyst for change.

Everyone feels like this at some point. It's not a sign that we need to shut ourselves away, punish ourselves or replay our trauma over and over. It's just a signal that we're pushing through something hard, and are having a very normal response to this challenge.

In fact, Dr Burgo says shame can prompt growth, and help build self-respect and pride — because sometimes shame has a lesson to teach us about who we are, and who we expect ourselves to be. Naming it for what it is, noticing it and feeling it without letting it consume us can be a revelation.

Have a conversation with it: 'Hello, Shame, my old friend. While I don't really want to be best buddies with you, it helps me to know that the intensity of feeling you evoke does not correlate with the degree to which I am a terrible human. I'm actually *not* a terrible human, and these supercharged shameful feelings are more a sign of sensitivity and humanity than a sign of failure. In fact, perhaps it's the very thing that bonds me to the rest of the good humans during a time when I feel very isolated ...'

Does this mean we need to reframe 'shame' to help ourselves feel better? I think it does. And I'm not the only one.

Dr Burgo says shame cops a bad rap — but if we can learn how to manage these feelings rather than run from them, or deny them, it will help us become more resilient in our lives, and feel better about ourselves.

Feeling foggy and stuck

You might spend a lot of time going about your day on autopilot and then collapsing into some kind of fog that involves trying to work out what you are meant to be doing now that you are:

a)
the saddest person
in your universe

b)
somehow expected
to forge a life that looks
different to before

Every day might feel like *Groundhog Day* as you try to avoid further disaster by keeping things routine. Setting your own reliable boundaries is a surefire way to stop other dumb crap happening, right?!

Indeed, these boundaries can become such a trusty defence mechanism that you will probably forget that the non-work part of your life is meant to include some lovely things you like to do. This is because of your:

a)
broken heart
and/or worried head,
obviously

b)
very important
meeting with
Netflix and a
fluffy blanket

The bad days. Yikes. They might not even take up a whole day. Or they might. The choice is *not* yours. Rough days are characterised by a tug-o-war going on inside your lacklustre self.

You *know* that you need to be strong, do something positive, keep moving, nurture yourself. But the reality is more pounding heart, eyes filling with tears, aching heart and racing thoughts. Sigh.

Know that these days — or part days — will come and go.

Know that it's okay to feel this way ... but also, please remember that if every day of the week is like this, for an extended period of time, then it's always a great idea to talk to a health professional about depression's constant looming presence in your life.

You don't have to settle into this bad day and give yourself over to it. Rather, think of it as an annoying sibling you want to elbow in the head when mum's not looking. Tolerate it, knowing that it will pass, and do the kinds of things that will help you to capture small moments of goodness. (Some simple little ideas to the right.)

Some quick ways to capture some moments of goodness

•

Eat the things you love the most, regardless of their perceived 'value'

•

Pat a pet

•

Make something

•

Get out in the garden

•

Binge-watch something escapist

•

Drink lots of relaxing herbal tea

Remember the three Ps

Psychologist Martin Seligman, the author of *Learned Optimism*, says that what he calls the 'Ps' can slow or stunt our recovery from difficult times:

Personalisation
The belief that we are at fault.

Pervasiveness
The belief that an event will affect all areas of our life.

Permanence
The belief that the aftershocks of the event will last forever.

Seligman's work has been centred on a sort of pragmatic positivity. He suggests that when going through tough times, we can look after ourselves a little better and set ourselves up for recovery by:

A

Being on the lookout for negative interpretations of events. We should fact-check these for accuracy, and create a more accurate interpretation if appropriate.

B

De-catastrophising — consciously making an effort to overcome the tendency to imagine worst-case scenarios.

C

Challenging our negative thoughts as they crop up, and reframing them in a more positive or accurate light.

Over and over and over!

Experts say there are ways to switch up your ruminations so they might actually do you good!

Do you find yourself stuck in the past — ruminating over all the awful little details, over and over and over again? Yup.

Fending off intrusive thoughts? All. Day. Long.

Being sidelined by memories popping up, and recoiling at how visceral they are? Argh.

Wondering how things could have been different? On the regular.

When things are grim, it's near impossible not to get stuck in a pattern of replaying what's happened to you — and indeed, the fallout you're navigating right now.

While ruminating, and torturing yourself with thoughts that you're mostly having simply in order to process the event, experts say there are ways to switch up your ruminations so that they might actually do you good.

It's called 'self-distancing' and honestly it makes a lot of sense — especially for those (like me) who are prone to constant self-blame, and flagrantly unkind mental self-flagellation.

Try these simple self-distancing techniques if you find yourself spiralling into rumination or intrusive thoughts. It can also be helpful to write down any insights that arise after using them.

The best friend approach

What would you say to a dear friend if they were navigating the same situation right now? How would you view them? What would you say to them?

The outside observer

Picture a fly on the wall observing what you're going through. What would they see objectively, without all the attached experience that your self-judgement brings to the table?

The future you

Provide fresh perspective by asking yourself, 'How will I feel about this a week from now? A month from now? Ten years from now?' Looking beyond your current situation can stop you disappearing too far down the rabbit hole of rumination.

Godspeed, little bunny!

Nostalgia: the urge to escape and the longing for long ago

Honestly, sometimes, when I was feeling really perturbed and in need of change, I swear I could feel myself floating out of my body and making a hopeful break for it.

Where I was going, I do not know, but the physical and mental urge to be far, far away was something to behold.

I couldn't stop thinking about places I went to and loved as a child. It was as if the safest place for my mind to go was way, way back to before I was an adult … before the hard things I was going through were even a twinkle in my eye.

Those places felt safe and secure and beautiful. The opposite of what my world was feeling like right then.

While nostalgia can sometimes make us feel worse, I kept rewinding my mind far enough back so that I felt better.

I thought about long walks in back paddocks picking blackberries to be made into a pie.

I remembered early icy mornings, getting up and quietly lighting the fire when I was far too young to do so. Sneaking about so nobody stopped me, and then proudly nodding when the adults woke up and asked if I'd made that lovely blaze.

I remembered climbing down cliffs to a blowhole — fishing rods over shoulders, pockets full of mints.

I remembered peering into a little bucket where a beautiful and tiny fish swam, then watching my uncle take him back into the sea and set him free.

It felt like my brain wanted to process some good things amidst the hard stuff. And it made me feel equal parts a bit better, and filled with longing for the places I used to be.

I guess I am telling you this because it might be something you are going through ... and perhaps the places you used to go to a long time ago might help you to find yourself a little more, too?

'When nostalgia is used in a healthy way,' explains psychology professor Dr Krystine Batcho, 'it can be like a crutch that grounds you in your past while you figure out how to move forward in a new situation.'

Nostalgia can help you connect back to the parts of you that have remained stable, giving you some sense of continuity in your life.

Indeed, researchers have found that reminiscing about happy events may increase positive feelings, and dampen the release of stress hormones after a stressful event.

By remembering the happy things we did as a kid, we can reinstate healthy emotions, such as being loved and feeling a sense of security, and create a sense of hope for the future.

Nostalgia can provide clues to how we might feel a little better — or at least a little more like ourselves.

As I pushed through my hard days, I found myself rewinding to simpler and happier times in my life — eating the foods I ate then, doing the things I did then, dragging out books I had read and music I had listened to.

I found myself buying lots of magazines — a habit I had mostly abandoned during the previous decade — and sitting at home on the couch drinking tea and soaking up the experience of enjoying pages a clever editor had put together.

I bought a CD player (*I know!*) and unpacked dusty boxes of old CDs, playing them with the windows open, nice candles burning, a bit more of a spring in my step.

I bought Boston buns, something I loved to eat when my own kids were little. (Did you know the original Boston Bun recipe has mashed potato in it? It's true.)

I ate cheese on toast. Tinned spaghetti. Crumpets with peanut butter. Stacks of toast cooked until very dark, little bit of butter, lots of Vegemite. These were all things I used to eat and they helped me feel much, much better. (More on food in Chapter 8.)

Out with the bad

For me, these nostalgic clues worked the other way, too. Things that reminded me of hard times were swiftly removed from my life. Sold online, the money diverted into fresh new things that didn't make me feel sad.

I sold my old Kitchen-Aid, which reminded me of the many hours I'd spent 'stress baking'. I replaced it with a new pink one that makes me happy every time I look at it and reminds me that I have a peachier new life ahead of me.

A painting that felt like it had some dark significance also got the boot. I used the money to buy a blender so I could make bolstering smoothies and start a new milkshake-making ritual with my kids.

Some ideas from friends who have been through hard times

As much as I wanted to communicate my own experience of dealing with tough times, I also wanted to share the views of others. So I chatted to a bunch of buddies and people in my circle about their own experiences of hard times.

I wanted to know what helped them, and what they would say to others who are looking for some light at the end of the tunnel?

"

This painful traumatic time *will* pass, and you *will* feel better one day. It may not be soon, but it *will* happen. You don't have to worry about how to get there or when you'll get there ('there' being the happy, easier life part), just know that it *will* come. All you have to do is get through each day, week, moment and nurture yourself as best you can in the meantime.

Sit in the corner and lick your wounds for as long as you need to. There's no time frame, you'll know when you're ready to leave the corner — when you feel there's more to life than siting in corners. Write your thoughts and feelings out, there's a magical process that happens when you look at those thoughts/feelings on a bit of paper — an invisible distance and perspective — plus it's cathartic and healing in a profound way.

Put it all down in the knowledge that no one will ever see what you write, pour your dear little wounded heart out in ink. Then one day, when you're ready, burn those writings in a fire and kiss them goodbye. Thank them for the lessons learnt (possibly with tears) and think about how far you've come since writing them. Burning the writings might happen a month later or it might be ten years later. There's no time limit. You'll just know when you're ready to do it." — **Hope**

"

I used to see things very black and white. It helped me have good boundaries in some ways, but was a handicap in others. Now I'm much less judgemental. You have no idea what people are going through; everyone has their own Greek tragedies to tend. Cutting other people slack has had the effect of making me so much less critical of myself. Perfectionism used to cloud my life, but now I'm better able to like and accept who I am, and most importantly to forgive my own missteps. I'm softer on myself and the world. That has been the greatest gift of the whole ordeal." — **MM**

"

I lost both of my grandparents in the same week. It was devastating. At the time, I did a lot of sleeping and felt pretty shit. Now that I am through the very darkest part of that grief, I am trying do lots of positive things like swimming and reading. Sometimes I still feel quite out of sorts." — **LF**

"

Grief is a peculiar beast. It pops up when I least expect it. Two-and-a-half years post break-up, I can say that it does get better. I had, er, complications in my break-up, too, and lost a dear friend, so it's hard to say which heartbreak fits in what box, but I cried rivers, had countless early nights and long baths and said 'No' a lot. My mantra was 'This too shall pass'. That was helpful, because when you're deep in it, you forget. Lately, when people ask how I am, I reflect, then smile and literally jump up and down realising that *Yes! I do feel good! Things are good.*" — **AL**

"

I was so heartbroken I couldn't feel anything else but pain. I really found it very hard to make decisions. For a while I had the feeling I wasn't important to anyone. A feeling I never had before …

I was glad I could go to work, it took my mind away from my feelings. But every day when I came home, I couldn't stop crying. I lost a lot of weight because of the way I felt. People told me I looked so good, but I'd never felt worse. After a year, my psychiatrist said it had been enough suffering. He suggested I should start taking antidepressants (again) and that was a relief." — **MvM**

"

Be very, very kind to yourself and take all the time you need, because … it won't always feel like this." — **Kate**

"

I remember the worst things about heartbreak was waking up really early; the pain and sadness would set in and I couldn't sleep. I found it hard to eat, too. It's hard to see a way out when you're heartbroken. But like everything, time helps. You need things to look forward to — book a little getaway with friends, just little things to keep you positive. You come out the other side a stronger and happier person. Battle-scarred, yes, but with renewed purpose and goals." — **J**

CHAPTER 3

Who even am I — and how will I keep going?

> 'The best way
> out is always
> through.'
>
> Robert Frost

PEOPLE WILL INVITE you places. You might not want to go. You might panic at the thought.

Honestly, that was me. I hardly went to anything for two years.

I was previously the sort of person who was around other people a lot. I had a shop, and before that a cafe. I ran a craft group, I ran workshops, I did talks about being creative and writing blogs and making time for nice stuff. I spoke on the radio ... I even went on TV.

But when everything got too much and I had what some might like to call an extended breakdown, the idea of living that friendly, chatty, visible life felt impossible.

It felt like I had lost myself and broken apart. The idea of someone peering into the broken bits of me seemed very scary.

Tucking yourself away

When people asked me along to things, I would mentally recoil as though they had suggested something that was incredibly agonising.

I would say no. Or sometimes I would say yes — but then go backwards and forwards in my sad swirling, trying to work out how to NOT go to the thing. As the event dawned closer, I would think of all the excuses:

A deer hit my car.

I have gangrene.

I broke. (Actual finished sentence.)

I have no words that will work in a social setting.

I am a monster. (Actual feeling of heartbroken person.)

Because the truth was, I felt like a monster, so unfamiliar was I with myself. Self-isolating seemed to be the best way to get a handle on life, slowly but surely.

The idea of going somewhere, as though I was my old self, seemed a sort of lunacy. I truly thought I looked like a completely different person. When people glanced my way, I was dead certain they were noticing the heartbreak in me — that it had turned me into someone else they would need to be introduced to all over again.

And maybe, in some ways, it had.

Apart from the me-looking-like-a-stranger thing, I was terribly worried people might ask me, 'How are you?'

One-on-ones with close friends were fine. They had seen me in my wretched monster state and I had seen them. I knew what would happen and that they were okay with monsters. And crying. They were okay with crying, too.

But the idea of being in a room with a few or even lots of people? Forget it. I was certain my pain would be visible, that the change in me would be obvious. That I looked completely different now, and people would point and stare.

Once, when I went out to a concert and ran into old friends, I scanned their faces to see if they were noticing the new me. They were certainly *looking* at me, but I couldn't fathom whether they were noticing me or the horrific monster I had become. I could feel tears welling as they chatted to me, but I pushed them away with a forced grin that looked more like a grimace.

Sometimes, I thought about pretending to be fine, but the idea of forcing a jolly face on my non-jolly self seemed too exhausting and I'd probably want to sleep for one million years afterwards to recover.

Once, I tried to convince myself that staying in alone on my birthday watching *Married At First Sight* and eating a bowl of tuna salad would be a great way to celebrate. I *almost* believed it. But not quite. #WorstBirthdayEver

Making friends with the 'monster'

When you are feeling fragile, you may find that you really want to be away from the fray, but when other people are not around or push on without you, it's an outrage. Confusing, *non*?

No, you don't really want to be social ... but could people please quietly invite you anyway each time they do a thing? Could they please include you or reach out without expectation anyway? Because it helps you feel less of an outsider, less like an excluded monster ... but you can still stay at home?

That's how I felt, at least.

This sense of being an outsider was very acute for me, and while I had felt it a bit at other times of my life, a serious dose of adversity supercharged it into something very potent.

Honestly, I do feel a bit embarrassed talking about this, because a tiny troll inside me is calling me a lunatic.

If you are feeling similar things, like you are abnormal in some deep way, rest assured you won't always be a secret feeling-filled creature from the dark. The early weeks and months recovering from any sort of loss are a complicated and shapeshifting biz, but things become less scary as time marches on.

I suppose it's a bit like when you go to the dentist and get an injection: in *your* mind, your face is swollen to the size of a piñata, but in real life, to most people, you just look like the regular old you.

REACHING OUT

If *you* find yourself isolating more and more, please let someone
help you. A trusted GP is a good place to start — or head
to a website such as Beyond Blue to find information
about getting in touch with a sympathetic counsellor.
Sometimes it's just too much and we need someone to
step in and short-circuit the struggle with some solid support.
See page 25 and head to Chapter 10 for information about
accessing practical support from professionals.

Generally, when you have had your heart broken into a zillion pieces, *most* other people don't notice it after a few weeks. They're often blissfully ignorant or they've simply moved on from the experience that continues to consume your life.

Very often, it's only your nearest and dearest who can see the cracks within. The rest of the world is so bogged down in its own dramas that people don't even notice there's a monster in the midst.

That said, it's perfectly okay to avoid, for a while, the sorts of social situations that strike terror into your heart. It's okay to slow things right down and allow yourself the time you need to feel human again.

Hurt humans need time to recover, rebuild and reacquaint themselves with the world, and this often needs to be done one tentative step at a time.

Don't expect too much of yourself. Pare things back to small gatherings, or even seeing just one buddy at a time. Tell your close friends you are feeling this way, and about the monster feelings. Let them know that if they could just be there, check in often and listen without judgement/unsolicited advice when you're together, that will help.

I found when I saw groups of friends, the people-pleaser in me would try to listen to all their advice and I'd go home and tie myself up in knots working out how to follow it all when really, what I needed to do was go at my own pace and work through each day in a way that made sense to me.

I didn't isolate myself, but I did have a good chat to *me*, and I realised that slowing things down was okay. Feeling better and getting better takes time. You can't stand around drumming your fingers and hoping it'll hurry up.

It's also good to know that the feelings of panic or hopelessness can sneak up on you, even when you think you might be mending. Know that this is totally normal, too — and not a relapse of some kind, but rather a reminder that you are a complex and sensitive being, and this 'healing' business is going to ebb and flow, and take its own good time. That's okay.

And the very notion of actually healing? Of getting back to your old self? Of ever recovering?

It's a complex one because after battling through tough times you'll be a kind of *revised* version of the old you. You may be carrying a fresh new scar or two — but scars are underrated, and often come with a dose of character and wisdom.

Heartbreak and loss hit like a tonne of bricks. They take so much from us. Stepping back from situations that might deplete us further or challenge us when we're already on a very wobbly footing seems like a smart idea to me.

Eff you, everyone. (Also I love you.)

As your world is flipped upside down, so your perspective may be, too. Where before you may have noticed the kind gestures and cutenesses life offers up, now your radar may have firmly shifted to notice danger, thoughtlessness or drama — all of which make you feel depressed, panicked or disappointed.

The events that got you to your sad place have now set the tone for how you move forward.

This is to be expected, of course — it's a kind of protective mechanism in a quest to avoid further disaster. A cynical force field around you so you can never again be hurt by other humans.

Normal, everyday situations can feel very threatening when you're in this vulnerable state. A trip to the supermarket, which used to feel like … a trip to the supermarket, might now feel like walking the runway during Paris fashion week in front of a sniggering crowd with all your feelings showing.

Opening emails might set your heart pounding as you anticipate all kinds of doom. 'Today is the day my work is going to realise they made a mistake giving me a job,' you might think. Or, 'Someone might have sent me some hate mail and I dare not look in case it's the straw that breaks the camel's back.'

Perhaps everything in you wants to hear some good news ... and yet the idea of conversing or connecting to others seems like courting further disaster that will send you tumbling even further into some emotional abyss.

Mostly, of course, the poor sods trying to get in touch with you simply want to tell you you've won a fortune from a Nigerian prince, or invite you to have a cup of tea, or ask you if you have finalised that draft report thingy you're working on. Or even just hear the sound of your voice.

It's often very lonely, treading a very rigid path as you try to keep your world from spinning further. You so *want* someone to understand you. You want someone caring to listen to you. To simply soak up a little bit of your sadness, because gee whiz, things are getting soggy all by yourself.

You ponder how great it would be to talk everything through with the right person. And yet, *not* talking about it seems less ... traumatising, because you feel dead certain that everyone in your life will drift away from your complicated self.

Of course, the best types of people won't drift away.

Saying something like, 'I'm finding it hard to spend time with people at the moment because the feelings and conversations it sparks are hard to handle' can be enough.

WHAT YOU NEED FROM YOUR FRIENDS AND FAMILY WILL BE UNIQUE AND PERSONAL TO YOU … BUT HOW ABOUT THE FOLLOWING?

- Just send me a hello now and then — not a 'how are you?'. I will tell you how I am, when I can.

- Yes, a basket of treats stealthily dropped on the doorstep sometime would be so nice.

- Please do send me a cheery letter — not pretending nothing happened, but not particularly focusing on it either.

- Can we go for a walk and *not* talk about *the thing*.

- A drive in the country without any 'so how are things?' sounds great.

- Yes, eating a cake and drinking gin and watching Korean variety shows with no expectation of 'talking

things through' is a good way of being around me right now.

- I would actually love it if you offered to come with me to my doctor's appointment / legal service / psychologist.

- Could I see you on my own terms while I'm feeling so fragile? Sometimes things change quickly and I need to be on my own, but not all the time.

- Organising for friends and family to help drop off an evening meal for a week or two while I'm feeling so low really would help me to remember how important it is to eat — and that I'm not alone in this.

This is not to say that you shouldn't talk to your nearest and dearest during your hard times, but rather that you don't always *have* to if it's proving really hard. And neither party has to feel bad about that. It's just where you might be up to at this point.

It won't always be like this. As time marches on, you will …

a)
slowly begin to get used to your new life

b)
begin to emerge as a 'new' kind of you.

As you do this, finding ways to do things with other humans without your world starting to tip is key. And doing those things, slowly-slowly, more and more is a brilliant path to moving through your tough time.

In the long term, not everything can be navigated alone. So keep an eye on yourself, and if you're noticing nothing is sparking your interest and you're not taking even the tiniest step forward, give yourself a hug and contact your GP or a counsellor or therapist for help.

More on non-harrowing ways to ask for professional help in Chapter 7 — and some ideas if you're worried about paying for therapy, or are too embarrassed or fragile to ask for help.

Dealing with the waves, the tears, the slush

One minute you're able to hold yourself together and can see the way forward; the next you feel like you're perched on a cliff, surrounded by worried puffins, sobbing your heart out and about to be washed away in a wave of your very own tears. Spinning or spiralling or gushing or slushing like an angsty granita.

I am sorry. I know, I know. I am sorry you are in this part of the broken-hearted life.

Because everything has suddenly changed, you might have shifted into autopilot and switched on a setting marked 'Doom'.

But I can tell you it won't always be this way.

PERHAPS YOU ARE FEELING SOME OF THESE THINGS:

- Panic — sometimes with a turbo boost of adrenaline.

- Fear and anger, performing a showy dance together.

- Lost and aimless — because it's all changed now, even the light …

- Extreme sadness — a lot of the time, and at the most inopportune times.

- Not recognising yourself when you look in the mirror.

- Hopelessness — because how will things ever be okay now that you've realised the world is *like this*?

- Like you could win the Crying Olympics.

- Like you've developed strong gut muscles from all the body-racking sobs.

- Unlikeable, and saying mean things to your unlikeable self.

What can you do about these feelings?

Give yourself time to adjust. Don't expect to feel okay or good or great — but be sure to notice those moments when you do.

Quite often, we try to shake off the awful feelings, distracting ourselves in the hope that they might go away ... hello booze, compulsive behaviours, drugs and other distracting pals! And honestly, sometimes you might truly need six glasses of whisky to help you push on through.

But generally, these are not things that are going to help, right? (No shit, Sherlock.) And in fact the whole idea of doing something that's not great for your body/mind, in a quest to edge away from your sadness, is a sort of folly.

Instead, it can be a good idea to treat yourself like a little kid. Allow the feelings to wash in and over you. Name them as they arrive. Trust that they will flow away if you just sit with them for a while.

That's not to say that you must spend your days under a blanket, wallowing deep in your difficulties. For sure, head out and do things that distract you and make you feel part of the world for a wee while. But when those big emotions come, don't feel the need to deny them or talk yourself out of that state of mind. A shit thing has happened and it's okay to take some time to come to terms with it.

If you're finding that your swirling thoughts or big feelings are all-consuming, it's a brilliant idea to give yourself a bit of a hand.

Some people find talking things through with someone trusty can help. If so, find a trusted friend or family member and do that.

Alternatively, if you don't feel the people in your life are able to hear about how you are feeling right now — for various reasons they may not be able to — or that there's not someone you can trust with the sort of feelings and details download you need to have, then finding a counsellor is a great idea. More about this in Chapter 10.

Don't expect
to feel okay or
good or great
—but be sure
to notice those
moments when
you do.

♥

Strategies for processing what has happened

The best way out truly is through, but there are many small ways you can anchor yourself, and feel a little less unmoored, as you find a way to do this.

Writing is one of those ways.

Writing it all down

When I was particularly broken, I wrote down many of the things I was feeling, as they happened. I just got out my phone and tapped them into my notes; I felt the urge to dump things out of my head so frequently that, for me, it simply wasn't always practical to scribble them in a journal. (Woe betide the poor bugger who finds my phone and manages to crack the code, because among my password reminders, bookmarked recipes and ideas about names for future kittens, they'll also find loads of teary rantings.)

For me, finding the words to express and record what I was going through somehow held comfort. It was like I was able to turn a swirling emotional twister into something that could be pondered from afar — as though feelings that felt more like a movement or a colour could be broken down to their essence and made more sense of.

Writing things down definitely has some weird but very real magic about it, where thoughts that might be trapped in a continuous loop in your head are siphoned out and exorcised. It's like releasing a pressure valve, or a kind of lancing, letting the swirling awfulness ease away.

When writer Joyce Carol Oates' husband died unexpectedly, she wrote a whole book, *A Widow's Story*, as she forged through her grief. As she explains, 'The act of writing is an act of attempted comprehension, and, in a childlike way, control; we are so baffled and exhausted by what has happened, we want to imagine that giving words to the unspeakable will make it somehow our own.'

This makes a lot of sense to me, because when I was feeling scared or anxious or hopeless, I felt compelled to write about it. This writing made some hard-to-understand feelings less confusing. It was also a way to look after myself, by paying attention to the difficult bits, and then pushing on with them in my waking life (or on the page/screen) — for the time being, at least.

Of course, not everyone wants to tap their darkest thoughts into their phone. Some will always prefer to pen flowy cursive or scratchy hieroglyphics onto an actual paper page. There's so much merit in that, too. Researchers tell us that in terms of cognitive development, there are clear benefits to writing by hand, as it requires multiple areas of the brain (ones relating to sensation, fine motor control and thinking) to become activated simultaneously, and this doesn't happen in the same powerful way when we use a keyboard.

Even recording your thoughts can pay dividends, so you could try cracking out your phone's voice-recording app.

Whichever method will most easily expedite your guerrilla journalling and encourage you to write often and promptly is the best one to choose.

The main thing is to just get cracking.

Concentrate on unloading your feelings and surrounding yourself with the things that comfort you a little during these dark days.

HOW TO JOURNAL IN 10 EASY STEPS

1. Set aside a small chunk of time; experts say 15–20 minutes three or four days a week is ideal.

2. Find somewhere private and comfy, so you don't feel awkward or self-conscious, or like you need to censor yourself.

3. Write freely and don't worry about making it pretty or perfect.

4. Don't worry too much about spelling and punctuation — this is for your eyes only.

5. Don't impose literary expectations on the way you write.

6. Write quickly and don't judge yourself or your words while getting them down.

7. If you're not sure what to write, try a 'stream of consciousness' or 'free writing' style, where you just write whatever comes into your head, without stopping.

8. Keep your output somewhere that feels safe and secure to you.

9. Think of your journal as a buddy who wants to hear your inner thoughts.

10. Take a break if journalling is not helping.

You may not want to write a novel, but writing something will truly help. Perhaps you will never read these notes again, but that doesn't make them any less valuable. This journalling is about getting down the bare bones of your thoughts and feelings. Taking time to document things you may not feel comfortable sharing with anyone else will lighten your emotional load, help you to feel a little less overwhelmed, and promote mindfulness, too.

Writing your way through

Look, I'm going to harp on and on about writing your way through hard times, because it's really *that* helpful.

Journalling can help us digest and metabolise our experiences, and the act of organising our thoughts helps to lighten the load on our brain, freeing it up to work on other things.

Not only does journalling allow you to process how you are feeling, remove cluttery confusion from your brain *and* give your relentless urge to ruminate a focus, it provides a helpful record of where you have been.

Seeing where you were, even weeks later, can help you notice the progress you are making when you actually feel like you're very stuck.

When done regularly, research has shown that journalling can even strengthen the immune system by helping to manage stress. It has also helped to improve the wellbeing of people suffering from conditions as varied as post-traumatic stress, trauma and insomnia.

So really, why wouldn't you put pen to paper?

Journalling is a therapeutic tool that is really easy to *start right now*, to help you feel like you're moving forward. And who knows, you might even scribble down some notes for your future best-selling memoir!

Why wouldn't you start writing, I ask you? Off you go. Come back to this page again later.

Gentle reminders: 6 go-to ways to process and push on

While this pain is still fresh and body-filling, the very best idea is to be as gentle and as quiet with yourself as you can.

1. Resting and slowing your life way, way down is ideal. Take it easy and be a bit gentle with you.

2. Crying can help. In the bath. In the shower. In your bed. In the car. Let yourself feel what you need to feel, especially if it's all building up. No need to hold it in and 'be brave'. Allow yourself to grieve and come to terms with the sad thing that has happened to you.

3. Distractions can sideline the ache for a tiny while, here and there. Perhaps a mindless binge-watch of a show you like? A deep dive into a book that takes you into a different time and place? Plugging into something that fills your ears with chatter or music or ideas? Sometimes, prescribing yourself these kinds of distractions really does work.

4. I found that paracetamol *really* helped too. See page 16.

5. For me, at the start, nostalgic comfort food was soothing and felt a bit like a hug. As time — and possibly too much comfort food — wore on, I moved on to 'good mood food', because I realised that hugging myself with food in the long term made me feel like I was living in a sort of quicksand-filled alternate universe. But food is good, so whatever works for you!

6. Just in case you missed it … *write it down.* All of it. Swirling thoughts are not only difficult to process, they can push you further into anxiety and depression. Writing down all the thoughts, feelings and challenging situations not only gets them out of your head, but allows you to review them at a later time and untangle how you feel. It doesn't have to make sense, look nice or even be legible. The main thing is to get things down and empty your already overloaded head, to help you patch up your heart a little, slowly but surely.

CHAPTER 4

Inching
forward,
day by day

You know what
they say, huh?

Admitting you
have a problem
is the first step
to sorting out
your situation.

GRANTED, WE'RE NOT deep in 12 steps here, but when you've been through a difficult experience, or are ensconced in it still, it can be ridiculously difficult to inhabit life in any way that feels remotely normal.

There is absolutely no need to shake off the hard stuff you are processing, because of *course* you are fragile or angry or overwhelmed or whatever your feeling may be. Give yourself a hug and remember that all this stuff can't simply be ignored away.

The feelings are there to give you clues, a kind of road map, if you can believe it — telling you where to apply a sort of 'feelings first aid', and what to prioritise as you go about getting yourself back on track. Looking carefully at whatever crappy feeling is washing over you is ultimately helpful, because it means you are taking the time to note what's *really* going on with you, and what might be motivating your emotional response.

Sitting with the feelings also gives you an opportunity to consider what might help you to feel more like *you* ... and mull over how your loss or difficulty has tilted you off balance.

Operating in a freaked-out or weighed down survival mode as your default is *not* going to help one little bit. But breaking down those big feelings and getting to their root causes — either on your own, with a trusted person or with a therapist — can help you 'unstick' yourself, inch by inch, and help you make small steps forward.

Adventure mode vs disaster mode

One thing that helped me was to learn a little bit more about acceptance and a lot more about belief in myself. I imagined myself during a less terrible time, and tried to think about how I'd fix things with admirable good humour and bravery.

It was a sort of *Charlie's Angels* response, if you will. Like pretending to be a sassy lady who can sort stuff out and punch the odd villain in the neck. This ...

a) didn't work every time

b) often lapsed mid-attempt!

But sometimes, the simple conscious act of trying to pull myself out of 'disaster mode' and into 'adventure mode' was enough to stop a spiral of panic or sadness or idiotic helplessness.

In a fragile or recovering state, instead of feeling curious or adventurous, you might be feeling really freaking freaked out — to a panicked sort of level that doesn't relate to the task or experience at hand. If you are feeling this way, you are not alone. Hugs to you.

When you are going through a hard time, you may feel that the ground is shifting constantly underneath your feet. You may respond to these shifts in ways that are unfamiliar, and ways you are perhaps not proud of, as you are struggling to come to terms with your new normal.

Know that your heightened, bonkers or bewildering feelings can often be traced back to some base feelings of shock and sadness at where you are now. It's like lots of little and big aftershocks after the original difficult thing. (Whose stupid idea was this, Universe? Sigh.)

When this was happening to me, I'd find myself saying 'What am I doing? Why am I feeling so breathless and talking so fast and loud, and why is my face so wet?' The answer was that I had simply been trying to hold it together for so long that some of the freaky stuff busted out. Sometimes this freak-out showed itself as fear. Sometimes as panic. Or worry. Or dread. Or disconnection. Or even anger.

If this sort of stuff is happening to you, my thoughts are with you. Know that this state of overreaction and out-of-proportion blowing is a temporary state. It will eventually end as you learn to shift your thinking.

One of the good things about overthinking is that you tend to get to the root causes of stuff much faster. When you feel something that seems to go from 0 to 100 way too quickly, remember that it's very rarely about the thing at hand. Chances are it's a deeper and more familiar feeling in disguise.

So if you are suffering from way-too-big dread, scary big panic, teary big anger, illogical fear of the post office — trace it back to the source, take a deep breath and know that you're mostly simply in pain again. Your dread, panic, anger is really just sadness and hurt.

Very quickly you will realise that feeling the sadness and hurt is actually a much simpler way to push forward.

What to do about fear, panic and (perceived) lack of progress

Firstly, stop measuring your new self against your old self or other selves. Know that this is an updated sort of you — one you don't yet have your head around and that is shifting all the time.

Secondly, take some time to think about what might work for you, as you decide how to inch forward.

It's totally okay to shrink your circle down for a while and not be social until you are ready. We talk about this in Chapter 6 a little more, and there are some ideas on how to broach your struggle with your pals.

If we're talking about having trouble at work and feeling anxious and unable to push forward ... that is harder. My advice is to give yourself some time and let your manager know you are struggling. If you're really concerned about your anxiety affecting your work, head off to your GP to explain that you've hit a rough spot and need some help to work through your panic and dread. A therapist can act as a circuit breaker and give you some strategies that will help you feel more secure in your professional life.

As a writer, I have always found my work to be a brilliant salve, because it's quite solitary. When I did have to deal with others, I very often found my heart pounding, and I worried disproportionately about making mistakes or not working hard enough. None of this was grounded in fact, and once I recognised that it was a pattern — that it was an anxiety response rather than a response based on the situation or my ability — things got easier.

A little bit of mindfulness goes a long way, so look for the patterns or habits your anxiety tends toward if you're prone to panic. Understanding these patterns can help diffuse things when you're feeling overwhelmed — and may even begin to make these attacks less potent, over time.

It's okay to slow things down for a while and just do the job at hand as best you can, and to take the time you need to feel better again. In the scheme of things, this recovery time is well spent and will make you a cleverer, more generous and more insightful person. Think of it as a slight sabbatical, and give yourself permission to slow down from the rat race for a while.

For some people, getting support from just one or two trusted pals or family members during these insular tough times is really helpful. Knowing someone has your back, knows you are not deliberately being a knotty-haired weirdo *and* unconditionally accepts you, makes a big difference. People like that are a beacon of goodness when things feel like a pile of shite.

In the end, there is no wrong way of dealing with hard times — *unless* of course we're talking breaking the law or intentionally hurting others or chugging dangerous amounts of booze and drugs.

Be kind to yourself and accept your own way of getting through your dark days. You are a brilliant and clever person who cares about you. You will edge forward, gather information, seek support in ways that make sense to you.

That said, if your tough time is pushing you to the brink of a mental health crisis, you *must not* navigate that alone.

If you had a heart attack, you wouldn't attempt to fix that yourself, would you? Same goes for a mental health crisis.

Remember, catastrophising sucks

Often, when things swirl out of control, we employ various misguided strategies in an attempt to wrestle back a sense of 'agency'.

Catastrophising is a biggie.

When we catastrophise, we operate from a sort of fearful siege mentality and imagine the worst-case scenario playing out in every aspect of our life. We go through everything that can go wrong and work through how these imagined challenges will impact on us. It's understandable, and seems very logical at the time — but it's also freaking exhausting and incredibly demoralising, and weighs heavily on the head and heart.

On edge, in this 'fight or flight' mode, it's easy to exacerbate our anxiety, escalate depression and foster a completely unwanted sense of hopelessness, which are the last things a struggling person needs.

Luckily, there are *lots* of things you can keep in mind as you find yourself doomsday prepping by default, to stop the catastrophe habit from taking on a life of its own.

Catastrophising stems from anxiety, and while you can most certainly look for logical ways to relieve worst-case-scenario thinking — such as writing down your worries or researching the likelihood of your worst cases happening — it's much more efficient to tackle the root cause.

When you find yourself imagining the crappiest outcomes ever, it's good to recognise that what you really might be seeking is actually a sense of feeling prepared and reassured.

Of course, imagining all the worst things does not actually mean you are prepared. Churning over every possible twist and turn is not the same as handling those twists and turns.

Usually it means you've just hopped on an emotional roller coaster and depleted your already flagging energy a little more.

Better to slowly work on putting yourself back together and feeling stronger, so that you can respond in more measured ways — on the spot — as life rolls out.

SOME OF THESE STRATEGIES MIGHT BE:

- Using an app such as CALM to help you find some equilibrium.
- Taking deep breaths — in for the count of four, out for the count of four, on repeat.
- Getting under a blanket and stepping out of the swirl for a little while.
- Hopping into a warm bath.
- Lying on the floor and stretching each part of your body.
- Talking to a pet or favourite person.
- Changing the scene — going for a walk, making something, going for a drive.

SOME HABITS TO KICK TO THE KERB INCLUDE:

- Google-searching bits of the catastrophe.
- Drinking three glasses of gin before work.
- Eating an entire packet of chips in 37 seconds.

Dealing with the anxiety and finding alternative ways to feel prepared and push on is the key to stepping out of this catastrophising cycle. Have a crack at feeling prepared simply by showing up and trusting yourself to respond to challenges.

Getting out of the swirl

Just noting that your catastrophising is an expression of anxiety will save you wasting precious energy thinking through imaginary scenarios. This is energy you can divert back into your good self and into anxiety-busting strategies instead.

I had been in the swirl of catastrophising for so long that it had become part of my DNA. No matter what I tried, nothing could short-circuit the fizzy, rushing, nauseous panic I was experiencing.

So I talked to a great doctor about how I was feeling physically and emotionally, and she explained that long periods of distress, sleeplessness and self-neglect were causing my body to not work properly. (It's a totally scientifically proven thing! See Chapter 5 for more on that.)

Thankfully, a prescription for some medication eased a good whack of my anxiety very speedily, and many of my physical symptoms as well. Talking to a psychologist helped a whole heap, too.

Probably as a result of my perfectionist streak, I'd been pretty concerned that taking medication for my mental health woes would impact me negatively, and I wouldn't be able to work, write or think like 'me' anymore. Maybe you've had those worries, too? I had to put those fears aside because I was simply not myself. I was crying all the time and in a constant state of panic. I was pretty peaky with sleeplessness, anxiety and depression steering my life.

Luckily, though, none of my concerns proved to be true. I wish I had realised earlier that some of my extreme feelings — chronic anxiety, debilitating depression, panic, fear — were sometimes indeed beyond my control, and not something I could overcome all by myself. I could have accessed the mental health support I needed a whole lot sooner and made my life *way* less anxious. Coulda, shoulda, woulda.

So, off to the GP and psychologist I popped, feeling even more sad and panicked as I did so. But it was a turning point, and things started to fall into place and feel more hopeful and achievable after that.

Turns out I had a lot of stuff going on, and I had zero hope of magically 'curing' myself. I needed some supportive professionals to guide me through so that I could start to move forward with my life again. Still, we live and learn.

Please be aware that you don't need to have fully blown post-traumatic stress disorder or meet a particular set of chronic criteria to get support for your mental health.

Experts suggest that if you are struggling with feelings that are overwhelming you or affecting your life in ways you'd rather they didn't, and you've been battling these symptoms for more than two weeks, you could really benefit from a kind doctor to offer some extra support and treatment.

And if you're still worried, think of it like this: if you sometimes need help for your physical health — which we all do — then you also sometimes need help for your mental health. It really is *that* simple. You would not avoid going to the doctor if you had a worrying physical health complaint (unless you are a bit of a twit like me), so it follows that you should not avoid going to the doctor when you have mental health concerns, either. Getting professional help is a brilliant way to bust the catastrophe cycle — and begin to feel less alone and better supported.

Making progress 101

Now that we've talked about breaking the catastrophe cycle, let's talk about re-learning how to push on in life, slowly but surely.

Making Progress: Simple Strategy # 1

LISTS, LISTS, LISTS

Make to-do lists to anchor you and help map your day — but don't beat yourself up if you can't achieve everything on the list, or indeed much at all.

Pushing through the day can feel like a giant to-do in itself, especially when people expect you to continue doing things like … ummmm … going to work, putting the bins out, keeping some food in the fridge. Frankly, it can seem like *a lot*.

But making a daily list of what you should, and would, like to achieve can be a total godsend when you feel it would be easier just to climb back into bed.

A list is a trusty pal that will give you some purpose when you've forgotten what the hecking heck you're here for. It can be a brilliant circuit breaker, pointing you in a fresh direction when thoughts are piling up in your head.

Studies have found that people who write detailed to-do lists before they go to bed sleep a lot better than people who don't — and the more specific the list, the faster they fall asleep. So if you have trouble getting to sleep or find yourself cycling through tasks and worries in your head at night, why not give it a go?

Making concrete plans — like writing a to-do list, or jotting in a journal — helps the brain concentrate on other things and stops intrusive thoughts interrupting.

Don't you want to rest your weary brain? *I knew you did.*

Excellently, you don't need anything fancy for this strategy, just a notepad and a pen.

And then the rule is simply this: write everything down and review the list each day, making adjustments or starting afresh.

Take note of what you have achieved, what you keep putting off, what you might want to scratch off the list, and whether you to reassess some bits.

Then, when people ask, 'Is there anything I can do?', you have a list right there — and they can actually help with things you are battling to get done.

At the very least you'll have a trusty record of the tasks that, once dealt with, will make your life run a little more smoothly. Even the act of dumping all the stuff that needs doing out of your head and onto a page is incredibly helpful in its own way.

And if all the things don't get done, that's okay too. We are usually brilliant enough to prioritise the things that matter most.

Really, getting it all on the page and feeling some sense of clarity is the goal here. Getting things *done* is a total bonus.

Making Progress: Simple Strategy #2

PRACTISE 3 GOOD THINGS

The 3 Good Things practice has been super-helpful for me, so perhaps you will take a shine to it, too? The idea is pretty self-explanatory and the benefits are far-reaching.

For 3 Good Things, you simply write down … three good things that you have experienced each day.

For optimal results, you are supposed to write about them in as much detail as possible, but I have found that even writing a very short sentence for each one still yields benefits.

On these pages, to the right, I've shared some of my 'good things' with you, as a simple example. Honestly, those things may not seem good to you, but they are good to me and that's the beauty of this practice. Your 3 Good Things are just for you, and you don't need to share them with anyone.

Some of my '3 good things':

1.
Noticed that someone had left two biscuits beside a public dog bowl when I was at the shops.

2.
Heard two old gents offering to shout each other breakfast.

3.
Did not leave the washing in the washing machine overnight.

As you can see, my 3 Good Things are very brief because I want to make this easy for myself and I'm seeking to do this daily.

The other beautiful thing about this simple practice is that it helps you look for life's gems. When you are feeling crappy, it's easy to cast the entire universe in a dark light — but 3 Good Things tends to shift that perspective to something brighter and provide a little optimism injection. You head into your day with a positive task in the back of your mind, more keenly on the lookout for the good.

If you practise 3 good things regularly, you can start to redefine the things that matter to you, which is especially helpful if you're feeling a bit stuck and anxious.

And science tells us the benefits can be profound. A 2005 study by psychologist Martin Seligman and colleagues, published in *American Psychologist*, found that writing about three good things was associated with increased happiness immediately after documenting the three things, as well as one week, one month, three months and six months later.

So, what have you got to lose?

Making Progress: Simple Strategy #3

RETHINK YOUR SCHEDULE

Researchers tell us that resilience is not all about having some sort of disaster-proof stoicism and being able to endure. Instead, it's how we take time to recover and regain our strength that plays a huge part when we're pushing through hard times.

Paring things back and giving ourselves as much down time as possible is super-important to optimise your recovery and make life more restorative. Anxiety and sadness take a toll physically. You will almost definitely feel exhausted, sick or fragile when you've had a rough day — so please give yourself some time to recover.

If you are finding yourself unable to sleep when you do lie down, try flicking on the radio, a non-dramatic podcast or a soothing audiobook. Honestly, there is something about voices that just lulls me to sleep, so maybe that will work for you, too?

Sleeplessness, intrusive thoughts, anxiety, confusion, sadness and more may all be interfering with your quest to get back on a more even keel, so it's important to address those challenges — with a professional, if need be — if you can. This might mean that you go and chat to your doctor about how hard things are, and perhaps get a referral to see a psychologist or counsellor.

Think about what your days look like, and how you're plodding along. Are you doing too much? Are you forgetting to block out a good wodge of rest time every evening? Perhaps you are spending time on tasks that don't matter so much right now?

The idea is to ditch all the things you don't really need to do — and instead make *yourself* and getting enough rest a priority.

> Ditching as many tasks as you can is an absolutely vital part of feeling a little more human, defragging your brain, and feeling more able to cope.

Also consider if there are some time-saving strategies you can implement to spare yourself some relentless jobs. Maybe get your groceries delivered once a week so you don't have to schlep to the shops. Maybe even a meal delivery service? Perhaps put all your bills on automatic direct debit payments, so you don't have to frig around worrying about them?

The idea is to get rid of time spent messing about doing tedious stuff so you can spend that time on looking after your weary body and mind. Resting and ditching as many tasks as you can is an absolutely vital part of feeling a little more human, defragging your brain and feeling more able to cope during overwhelming times.

Resilience is nurtured by trying, and then resting, and then trying again.

So take a breath, pare things back and make resting your precious and brilliant self an absolute priority.

As Reese Witherspoon, actor and producer of the brilliant film *Wild* remarked after her divorce from Ryan Phillipe, 'You know, you can't really be very creative when you feel like your brain is scrambled eggs.'

Comforting to know that after taking time out for a little unscrambling of the eggs, it is indeed possible to come back better than ever.

Making Progress: Simple Strategy #4

ENJOY NEUTRAL TIMES

One of the best things about 3 Good Things (see Making Progress: Simple Strategy #2) is that it teaches you to see the world through more hopeful eyes, which can be useful when you're feeling bereaved, heartbroken or unwell.

My experience has taught me that this reframing is a very important tool for pushing on.

Expecting the worst and being constantly primed for negative encounters is simply no way to live.

Living in survival mode, fearful of what's next, is not only exhausting, but adds a whole other layer of pain to our tough times.

Better to try returning to a more 'neutral' state, where you can slowly start to unpack any new trials and tribulations, and recast these in a different light.

By a 'neutral' state, I mean a state in which you are sorting your self-care and coping strategies so you can have some periods in your day when you feel simply okay … and not totally crap.

I understand that neutral is *hard* when you're feeling incredibly sad or under siege. But as time ticks on, and you begin to understand how your own grief, sadness or struggle affects you, you may catch longer and longer glimpses of this calmer state.

Soak this up and notice it. In my experience, the more you acknowledge and appreciate the calmer times, the more restorative they can be. And the more often they pop up.

You can
cross bits out.
Or redraw it.
Do it your
own way.

Making Progress: Simple Strategy #5

CREATE A 'ME MAP'

You might already know what a mind map is? It's a sort of diagram with a central idea in the middle and then lots of other related ideas drawn around it.

What I want you to do is make is a 'Me Map'. It's a way of accounting for the tasks, thoughts and issues you are having in a visual sort of way — and then drawing lines between them so you can work out what the heck to do next.

The idea is to put yourself at the centre of it, and all around the map you simply scrawl all the things that are affecting you right now. You can add to it over the days or weeks or months. And you can cross bits out. Or redraw it. Do it your own way.

The idea is to form a plan that accounts for the steps you need to take, the hurdles that are in front of you, and the progress you want to make. Because perhaps you have no hecking idea of where to next?

When I was at my lowest, I found it near impossible to work out where to begin. Some tasks I didn't dare put on my to-do list because they seemed so anxiety-inducing, and I simply felt incapable of getting things done.

Some of the tasks were big — like sort out finances.

Some of them were small — post that package that has been sitting on the table for two months.

Very often, I couldn't work out what order to tackle things in. Crappy times had taken a toll on how I processed information, and when I tried to work through stuff in my head, it felt like my brain was in a vice. A sort of adrenaline-charged vice.

Many tasks felt much more complicated than they really were due to my anxiety, sadness, fear, fatigue.

But luckily the idea that even the tiniest attempts at progress can cause movement stuck with me — and tiny, wobbly steps I took.

What helped to inch me forward was writing each tricky task onto the middle of a blank sheet of paper, and then scribbling all the elements that made up that task around it.

Capturing all the moving parts of a task I had to complete helped me work out what bits to do when, and identify which bits relied on other bits to be done before I got to them.

If that makes sense.

Basically, I drew the world's messiest and most disorganised flow chart. I then pulled out the steps that mattered and diarised them into days of the week or times of the day. It was cathartic to see it in black and white, and it helped to jumpstart those rusty processors in my old noggin and stop me avoiding things that needed to be done.

I know this idea might sound basic, but when you have had your world turned upside down and your heart shaken out of your pockets, or your spirit depleted by challenging times, nothing is as basic as it should be.

When we are so deep in our tough time, and so used to feeling anxious, we sometimes need to be reminded of how to progress.

Finding a way to get stuck into ignored or 'too-hard basket' stuff can help shift other parts of life more easily, too. When one thing becomes unstuck, other good things also start to flow. We gain confidence, and might even feel a little bit more resilient as we watch ourselves progress. Getting one thing untangled can encourage us to untangle the next gnarly bit, if you know what I mean?

If you are feeling like there's lots of hard stuff to tackle, sketching out a Me Map might just help you coax a lot of to-dos from their knotty storage spot in your head and heart, and allow you to look at them — and think about where to begin.

Please don't be at all surprised if it makes you feel horrible to write it all down. If it does? Honestly, stop. Take a break. Do it another time. Nobody wants you to feel terrible, least of all me.

Come back to it another day. Call in reinforcements and take this book with this page open to a dear friend, family member, or a professional who helps care for your mental health.

For many of us, our crisis has meant we are facing not only grief or heartbreak, but also other woes that are legal, health-related, financial, work-related, involve other people in our lives, or affect the roof over our heads.

Although you possibly feel like putting your head in the sand, under a pillow or between your knees, it can help to unravel these sorts of things on a big piece of paper with a strong cup of tea.

And even if you don't start acting on the Me Map that I am encouraging you to scrawl down straight away, writing down all the elements and starting to organise them into some logical steps and a timeline is a brilliant first step.

It's pushing forward, by small degrees — but progress is progress, after all, and another small step on the path back to wholeness and healing.

Another small step on the path back to wholeness and healing.

Getting your head a little bit more together

THE PROCESSES AND decisions that you once hardly thought about might now be a challenge — but don't despair, you are among friends.

Here are some simple ideas to help get your days back on track.

Try some anxiety-busting strategies

Okay, science tells us that when we are anxious, the part of our brain that helps us regulate our emotions and make decisions — our pre-frontal cortex — turns off. This is the part of the brain that helps us plan, process consequences rationally, and think logically.

Our pre-frontal cortex calms down our amygdala, the more hot-headed, instinctive, raw, impulsive, 'fighty and flighty' part of our brain.

So, to make wise choices we need to make sure our old PFC is switched on.

But how to calm the anxiety and give rational thought a chance to shine?

Well, some mindfulness and simple breathing techniques exercises are a good place to start, and the following ones work well for me.

Breathing exercise #1
The 'Let It Go'

- Choose a comfy spot and sit as naturally as you can. As you breathe all the way in, count to six. Now breathe out slowly counting to eight as you do. Try to relax on the out breath as much as possible, relaxing your shoulders, back and neck.

- Repeat: breathe in slowly and deeply to a count of six ... then breathe out slowly, relaxing to a count of eight. We want the *out* breath to be the hero, the part of the exercise where you let it all out and go a bit floppy.

- You can do this exercise at work, or on a train or in a waiting room. It's very portable.

Breathing exercise #2
The Balloon Belly

- Lie comfortably with your back straight and body as relaxed as possible. Put one hand on your chest and one on your belly.

- Imagine there is a balloon in your belly. Breathe in to inflate the balloon. Breathe out to deflate it. Your belly should rise and fall with your breaths.

- This is a good technique for home, perhaps before bed or in the morning when you wake up. Possibly not one for the bus ... but you do you, champ.

Breathing exercise #3

The 'Let It Go' With A Twist

- Try the Let It Go technique lying down. Feel your body pressing into the floor, mat or mattress as you breathe in for a count of six. Let your body relax and go floppy and floaty as you breathe out for a count of eight.

Breathing exercise #4

The Balloon Belly With A Twist

- Try the Balloon Belly exercise when you are *not* lying down. Inflate your balloon with your inward breath, and deflate it with your outward breath, as you sit in your car, at your desk or at the kitchen table.

When I'm anxious, I feel as stiff as a human ironing board, and completely forget that humans need to use their diaphragms to breathe, rather than sipping the air around them like lizards.

Taking deep and regular breaths makes me feel more connected to myself and a little less hopeless in two seconds flat. It reminds me to make friends with my body and situation, rather than resisting, fighting, tipping into anxiety and forgetting to ... you know ... breathe.

So, have a look again at the previous page and let's begin. Simple breathing exercises can help to dull some of those stress responses, or even turn them off.

There's lots more on everyday mindfulness in Chapter 11, but I wanted to slip the notion in here, too, in case you only get this far in the book. (No judgement, I know you have a lot going on!)

You could also try other anxiety-busters such as taking a long bath or shower, some gentle (or non-gentle, if you prefer) exercise, tucking yourself into bed and listening to an audiobook or focusing on something creative that grounds you.

There are also brilliant mindfulness apps that can prompt you to slow things down and pay attention to your body and breath, staving off the swirling thoughts or anxious fizz.

Write it down and sleep on it

More writing. I know, I know.

It's just that writing really *does* have superpowers, helping us get things off our chest — or out of our rattled brains — and onto a page, where they transform from swirling thoughts into more tangible, and possibly even tackle-able, things.

As my great-grandfather Frank W. Boreham — author of a slew of books and writer of thousands of editorials for *The Age* and *The Mercury* newspapers, once said:

> We invariably find ourselves richer on rising than we were on retiring. Personally, I have spent most of my life scribbling. I have always found it a mistake to attempt to complete a manuscript in one day. I like to do part of it — enough to get the theme well on to my mind — and then go to bed with the work half-done. I do not consciously review the matter during the night: yet I invariably wake up with a batch of ideas that were not there the previous day.
>
> I have always kept a notebook beside my bed in which to record, as soon as I opened my eyes, the treasure with which my plunge into oblivion had enriched me. How often a word or a phrase or a quotation eludes us overnight; but in the morning it seems to be standing in the gateway of consciousness awaiting us.

Never underestimate the power of your subconscious to mull things over as you snooze, and to cast a different perspective on them when you wake up.

How do I sleep though?!

It's pretty hard to have a level head when you've only managed to grab a few solid hours of sleep before waking up in a cold sweat or panic or nightmare-induced state.

Night time becomes something to be endured — a time dotted with attempts to distract yourself from your own distress. And then, when you're awake, you're foggy, which makes lucid decision-making pretty impossible.

Research tells us that disturbed sleep is a core feature of grief, post-traumatic stress disorder and depression.

Your amygdala is fight-or-flighting like a frog in a sock — *and* your body is processing your experiences in all kinds of physical ways. There's a whole army of cells and a barrage of responses at work inside you. No wonder you're so darned tired/wired!

That said, all these responses are designed to ensure you survive, as humans have done for millennia. So while you might feel like punching your primitive instincts in the neck, it's kind of interesting to note that these responses are ...

a)
normal and natural
(if difficult to deal with)

b)
signs your body is rooting for you and wants you to not only survive, but thrive.

If only you could get some sleep, things might get a little clearer, and the world might seem a little less hostile, right?

But how?

The experts tell us that a concept called 'sleep hygiene' is key.

Restful sleep is so essential to our physical, mental and emotional wellbeing.

Easy ways to sleep easier

We talked about some sleep-inducing tricks a little earlier in Chapter 1, but let's go through some of these again in case you're too sleep deprived to find that bit.

Talk to your GP. Do it. Let them know that you're not sleeping and they can develop a treatment plan that will reassure you, make you feel a little more like yourself and hopefully allow you to get some sleep in the process.

Don't worry if you can't fall asleep — read a book, get up, do some stretches. Don't put too much pressure on yourself to succeed. Just switch it up and try again a bit later.

Phew. Maybe you are asleep right now after reading so many better sleep rules? Sorry to be bossy. Just cherry-pick those that make sense to you.

And because restful sleep is so essential to our physical, mental and emotional wellbeing, we'll come back to it again in Chapter 7.

OTHER SLEEP-PROMOTING TACTICS:

- Help your body find its own rhythm by waking up at the same time each day.

- Keep electronic devices out of the bedroom.

- Keep your room dark and calm, and at a coolish temperature. (Maybe reduce any clutter if you have the energy? A tidy room helps me sleep less guiltily.)

- Try to get in some exercise during the day to tire yourself out a little. Sometimes all we can manage is cruising the aisle of the supermarket, or sweeping the kitchen floor, but honestly those things count.

- Avoid booze and caffeine. *I know this is hard.* I'm just going to leave it here. You are a grown-up and you will sort this out for yourself. Or, if you can't, chat to your GP about this.

- Take a shower before bed. A nice shower really does act as a circuit breaker and will help you relax. Bonus points for taking some time to look after yourself, too.

- Try drinking warm milk — or warm almond milk — before bed. There is nothing wrong with treating yourself like a toddler some of the time.

- Make sure you are wearing (or not wearing) whatever feels good to you in bed. Don't climb into bed wearing the clothes you wore all day! It's against the rules.

- Don't binge-watch shows until 2 am ... especially if you have to get up at 6 am. And avoid disturbing content. Watching and reading terrible things is only going to amp up your anxiety and have you tossing and turning.

Phone a friend

There is something clarifying and cathartic about putting words to your current dilemma and hearing them said out loud. Very often, just talking about things — rather than mulling them over in a to-and-fro state in your addled brain — helps you distil the situation down to its bare bones and settle on an appropriate way forward. Or at least *a way forward*. Any way forward!

Many of us will have a buddy or a family member who can lend an ear when we're working through a personal crisis and help us decide where to next, and how.

This is honestly one of *the best* ways that friends and family can really help — with tangible and practical things.

That said, asking for help can be pretty blinking hard.

But, as you teeter on the brink of reaching out to someone trusty, remember that this is just what all those people who have been saying 'Let me know if I can do anything?' are waiting to hear.

They *want you to ask.*

They want to hear you say, 'I need help with (insert thing here)'.

Because then they can say, 'I can help with that. Let's muddle through it together.' Or even, 'I know exactly what to do.' Or perhaps, 'I have a discreet friend who is an expert in this field.' Or, 'I am so glad you told me and I'm here to support you.'

Talking to a trusty person about what you need help with — whether it's your living situation, your finances, your mental or physical health, legal matters or other important life-affecting stuff — is the first step to getting a partner in crime to forge on with.

Make a shit list

When you are working through difficult feelings — sadness, anger, powerlessness, bitterness, rage, disbelief, confusion, resentment — it helps to make them a bit less abstract.

Why are you feeling like this? What are the exact things that are driving you to transport yourself into a sobbing and/or seething wreck?

Okay. It's *mostly* all due to the catalyst of your heartbreak. I totally get that. But let's get down to specifics. Let's vent in a super-safe place.

Take a pen and paper — or open the notes function on your phone or computer — and start getting it all out. You don't have to create the sort of poignant prose that made Virginia Woolf a household name. I'm talking about a simple list of the shit consequences of this situation. Get all the shit things down.

As you write, please know that this is a case of getting the worst stuff out of your head, and diminishing the emotional weight you are carrying around in your physical being. It's not a case of 'poor me'. Every single thing you write down represents one less thing *inside* you.

Write, write, write. Get down all the specific things that you are feeling like you have lost, or are missing out on, or are being unfairly dealt your way.

MAYBE IT'S THINGS LIKE:

- Loss of income due to not being able to work due to heartbreak.
- Feeling like nobody knows me anymore, because nobody knows what to say.
- My person left me all alone.

- I can't stop crying at inopportune moments.
- My face is always puffy and I don't know myself when I look in the mirror.
- I can't eat. I'm too sad. Nothing tastes right. I can't be bothered to make anything. I'm starving.

MAYBE IT'S THINKING THOUGHTS LIKE:

- Now I can't go on holiday with my person, or they took all my favourite records, or they are gone and now I'm here living my worst life.
- I don't remember how to be me anymore.

- I've lost my companion and now I don't know where to go or what to do.
- I just feel really blinking lonely.

Maybe it's other things.

Your heartbreak situation will have its own unique challenges.

Every time you find yourself in your head, with thoughts of how terrible it all is, *write it on your shit list*.

This list is not for you to mull over with a box of tissues and feelings of hopelessness. It's purely a tool to document and extract the day-to-day impact of your now-different life, and stop your poor brain and body overloading.

Very often, we feel embarrassed or ashamed about our circumstances and feelings, and we leave this giant clump of overwhelm inside ourselves. This does nothing to help us feel better, and indeed it probably makes us feel *much* more anxious and unable to cope. And then we feel even more embarrassed and ashamed of our frailty.

Use the shit list to extract the worst of what's going on with you. And even the not worst. Get it all down. Mention it all!

As you go through this process, you will not only start to feel a bit less bewildered by the giant clump of overwhelm, you may also start to feel less angry or anxious.

Your shit list can also be a great starting point for an honest chat with a counsellor or therapist. You can skim over it with them and talk about what's happened, *plus* all these shitty things that are making your life feel very, very challenging. They will have helped other broken-hearted souls navigate through difficult times before, and your shit list can be a sort of handy cheat sheet to get you both started.

However your circumstances are weighing on you, getting the worst of it out of your head is a brilliant way to relieve some of the pressure you are under.

(PS: Sorry this is happening to you. X)

Call in a professional

Truth be told, as much as we would all like to, we don't always have all the answers. And we might not always have a trusty person to help us through.

This is when it's a brilliant idea to find yourself an expert type who might be able to help.

The kind of expert help you access can depend on where you live, and perhaps on your financial resources. And also your ability to even ask for help, let's be real.

But guess what? Asking for help — especially from a professional — is one of the *best ways* to move forward and begin making the decisions you are finding tricky.

It's very easy to get stuck in the trap of thinking that you can sort yourself out if you try hard enough. But often, problems are simply bigger than us and our expertise. It's not a failing to call in the reinforcements; it's actually a huge strength, as well as a huge relief.

As I mentioned earlier, it took me a very long time to realise I simply couldn't DIY myself into a better situation. But once I'd enlisted some cluey types to support me — in my case an accountant, a new very kind GP and a psychologist — things began to get sorted out.

Recruiting some helpers reminded me *not* that I couldn't 'magic' things better on my own, but rather that I was strong enough — eventually! — to hoist a white flag when I needed to.

Perhaps you're a little like this, too, in one or more areas of your life?

The good news is that inviting someone expert-y into your 'mess' makes everything feel a little less unpredictable *and* helps you work through the decisions you need to make methodically.

Head to Chapter 10 for more on getting professional help, what it feels like to see a psychologist, and what a psychologist would like you to know about the experience of therapy.

Aim for a steady state

As much as happiness and joy are touted as the ideal, there are other helpful things to strive for when those seem so very far away.

Truth be told, when you've been through a terrible time, happiness and joy can feel a bit impossible. At this precarious point in your life you probably aren't saying, 'I want to be happy again!', but rather, 'I wish I could feel okay', or even, 'I just want to have an okay day.'

Aiming for a 'steady state' is a great option when life is crap. It's also a brilliant vantage point to start to form plans for the future.

One useful biological concept I stumbled across is that of 'homeostasis' — a state of physiological equilibrium inside our bodies that our inner organs and self-regulating bodily processes are constantly striving for.

Okay, that's quite the dry definition, but I think there's something in this *home-eee-ohhh-stay-siss*. (Say it with me!)

And while science-y people use it to refer to a biological state, I'd like to view the concept a bit more broadly, to refer to a state of being in which we feel both physically and *emotionally* safe.

A state of equilibrium is something to aim for if Being Happy seems a little lofty and extreme.

And while a steady state might sound like a low bar to set, aiming for it is a brilliant goal when you're remembering how to be a functioning human again.

Steady can help restore and strengthen your weary self.

This in turn can lay the foundation for more positive feelings, so you can amble through your days feeling less under siege.

Sure, for a while it'll probably be a case of two steps forward, one step back. Some moments things feel steady and a little more together — and then suddenly you're deep in the gloom again. Sometimes, the gloom just sneaks up on you. Other times it doesn't even sneak. Sometimes it just falls out of the sky and doesn't even *try* to be sneaky! Bastard gloom.

I know it might seem safer to simply settle into a familiar spectrum of sadness, not letting yourself feel too many happy feelings. The (incorrect) logic here is that at least when the crap and gloom hit, you're already primed for them, and the hits don't feel as surprising.

But remember this is just a defence mechanism — a way beleaguered humans deal with sustained stress. Let's think of it as a misguided form of resilience: a slightly bonkers way of protecting ourselves enough to push on.

I guess the thing to realise about these perceived 'steps back' or setbacks is that they're really *not* steps backwards.

I know, I know. You don't believe me.

But honestly, all of the feelings — and the awesome/crap waves they tend to dump on us — are just the way it is right now.

If you've had a setback, it's perfectly understandable, so try not to judge yourself.

And try not to panic.

But what if I did panic?

Notice your panic, then stop and take a deep breath, or even a few deep breaths (see the simple, calming breathing techniques earlier in this chapter).

Think of a way to step away from that panic cycle for 10 minutes and create some distance and relief. Give yourself some time to settle down and feel a bit more like yourself. Then, ask yourself a few questions:

When things are feeling quieter, take pen to paper and document the challenge. Start working through the logical elements bit by bit.

Whatever the problem, just chip away at it, and work through it accordingly.

Taking small steps to resolve or reset things is key.

What might help to fix this?

Who can help to fix this?

What do I need to do to feel like I'm managing the issue at hand?

What sparked this?

What is my first step forward?

When memory plays tricks ...

We don't really hear a lot about how stress, anxiety, depression and other mental health conditions affect memory, but it's a thing.

I once had a very sharp memory and could recall things, events, people and places so clearly it was annoying for those around me.

But as I worked through my own challenges encompassing trauma and loss, my memory faltered dramatically.

And not just my short-term memory, but my long-term memory, too. I can watch a whole season of a TV show on Netflix, but I will probably only remember three things from that series. And even then I will doubt my memory.

It's not just useless binge-watching details I lose. It's lots of things. Stuff I've done with the kids, childhood memories, things my children have told me lately, plotlines in books, song lyrics, chores I meant to do.

I'll forget I've completed a task and go back to do it again. I'll forget the details of arrangements I've made, even after I have checked them twice.

It feels like a weird combination of overload and anxiety, and it feels like crap.

Other moments, events, people and places, though, play over and over again when I am awake and also asleep.

It's like my brain has decided that because some memories must, for some reason, be repeated endlessly, there is no room for others.

And I don't really get to choose the ones I lose. Nor lose the ones that replay.

Maybe this sounds a bit like you, too?

When we're stressed, our adrenal glands release a hormone called cortisol. Studies have shown that having chronically high cortisol levels can impair memory — as can having a poor diet.

However, the good news is that you can reverse these effects by implementing some stress-busting strategies and caring for yourself. Which you are already doing — because look, you bought this book!

Foods containing plant flavonoids (such as those found in fruit, dark chocolate and even red wine!), omega-3 fatty acids and vitamins E and B appear to be beneficial for the parts of the brain that deal with memory.

So, what should you be stocking up on at the shops, apart from small amounts of red wine and dark chocolate? Have a look at the menu box on the opposite page for goodies to add to your next shopping basket.

And one last very easy way to improve your memory?

Drink lots of water! About 73 per cent of your brain is made up of water. When your brain dehydrates, it shrinks a little, affecting concentration, attention, alertness and short-term memory — and just a 2 per cent decrease in brain dehydration can diminish your cognitive skills.

So maybe you're not even that forgetful. Maybe you're just very, very thirsty.

Memory menu:
eat these foods!

To give your brain and memory a natural boost, make these items a regular part of your diet.

- Berries, apples, grapes, blackcurrants, pears and citrus fruits are all rich in brain-boosting flavonoids, as is dark chocolate (with a high cocoa percentage).

- As for B vitamins, great sources include bananas, beans, lentils and brown rice.

- Foods rich in healthy fats include avocados, olive oil, walnuts, full-fat yoghurt, coconut oil and fatty fish such as salmon, mackerel, sardines, anchovies.

- Eggs are a classic all-rounder, serving up omega-3 essential fatty acids and B vitamins.

- And don't forget green leafy vegetables, which are rich in magnesium and vitamins B, C and K.

- There's no harm stocking up on a few herbal helpers. It turns out rosemary lives up to its reputation for remembrance and is good for alertness. Why not burn some rosemary essential oil, grow some rosemary in a sunny spot or pop some in a vase, so you can breathe in the fragrance every time you pass by? Use fresh rosemary in your cooking, or add some to your evening bath. Some people even put rosemary sprigs in their cordial or gin and tonics!

- Sage, ginseng, lemon balm, mint tea and gingko biloba have also been shown to have positive effects on mental performance.

CHAPTER 6

Dealing
with family
and friends

> The support
> of friends and
> family plays
> a vital role in
> providing some
> protection from
> the fallout of
> terrible times.

SOME OF US ARE lucky to have friends or family members who are on the doorstep offering support when we most need it, with a trusty shoulder and a packet of tissues/bottle of wine/bag of Chinese food.

It's often very hard for others to know how to best respond when things are a bit shitty. Their 'Let me know if I can do anything' plea is pretty much the default method of support modelled to us, and as we know, a person in crisis often has *no* idea which thing to say in response to this.

You might just find that your difficult situation can be complicated even more — unwittingly — by the way others respond to you during this time.

I think this confusion around how to support someone having a hard time results in people doing nothing ... drifting away ... or doing/saying too much ... I remember hearing about the poet Charles Bernstein, whose daughter Emma died unexpectedly; he said the most welcome or helpful thing people would often say is, 'There are no words'.

Close friends might find your hard time a challenge. Friends you thought were more distant might step up to the plate. Some connections grow stronger, while others get put on the backburner.

Like I said, confusing.

You can choose to have a lot of feelings about this, but honestly? It's more tough stuff you don't need right now. Park it, I say. Concentrate instead on what you are going through, and know that hard times are hard for everyone, that other people's responses should not be looked on as a test of their loyalty, and that everyone will do the best they can do.

Even if their best doesn't seem to hit the mark, try not to get swept up in judgements or conclusions. That's just more drama and heartache you don't need.

Doing what you need to take care of yourself and keep things as stress-free as possible is what matters most.

Not everything has to be a negotiation or issue right now. Just note how things are for the time being, find a way to accept that 'it is what it is', and push on.

It's really easy to project our current struggles onto other people and make *them* our struggle. But let's not do that.

You can come back to the people you are struggling with later, when you are stronger, and can assess things with a clearer head. Perhaps you will strengthen those connections. Perhaps you will give lots of hugs and dumplings to people who have helped a lot. Perhaps you will forgive people you felt didn't step up. Or see that they tried, but you were not ready to see …

You can decide all of that later. Don't add any more chaos to your life right now. Instead, notice which people are easiest to spend time with, and do just that.

There's also the possibility that your friends might drift away because you're not able to let them in on what you're going through, as Matt Haig, author of *Reasons To Stay Alive*, found when he had a serious mental health crisis.

Matt says it wasn't actually because they were terrible friends, but because he withdrew so heavily from them and wouldn't return their calls, they weren't really aware of what was going on.

Matt's experience mirrors mine. It's pretty hard to talk to everyone in your circle about how hard things are. And what are people going to think if you are unable to respond or show up for them, or give them the time friendships need?

They are going to think you have other priorities. Priorities that are not them.

Here are some things to consider as you navigate your crisis and deal with the friends and family in your orbit.

Coping with people who want to 'fix' your sadness

Oh, the advice. It will roll in like a freakish wave, with you a tiny person clinging to a life raft, ill-equipped for the conversation that lies ahead, and even more ill-equipped for the sneaky whiplash you'll suffer as a result.

It's brilliant that people want to help. I, for one, really love it. I love that intention so freaking much.

What's not brilliant is that difficult life situations are so nuanced that 'out of the box' advice or judgements very rarely apply. The problem with advice is that it can often leave the struggler feeling misunderstood, judged, and/or confused.

Advice can ring in a sad person's ears for days, weeks, even months as they try to slot the pieces of their life back together and accommodate some of what's been said. A particularly jarring sentence may stay stuck in their mind for years.

Rather than containing the most insightful truths, sometimes the advice that is offered so genuinely merely mirrors the biggest assumptions the well-meaning person has made, or is an oft-heard phrase from a self-help book or movie.

These kinds of trotted-out responses often make the person giving the advice feel empowered. Let's face it, it's horrendous not being able to help someone you care about when they're having a crap time. Offering advice feels like a great way to lend a hand.

But such advice can often make a struggling person feel even more isolated, and doesn't help the giver or receiver as much as either would hope.

I don't bring this up to critique the advice-givers. Rather, I want to let you know that if getting advice is making you feel *worse*, not better, it doesn't mean you are weird. It means you are human and you need to be listened to — not told.

If advice has you rehashing things in ways that make you feel a bit panicked or re-traumatised as you relive dark days ...

If advice has you feeling like you need to comply with someone else's plan for you, or be rejected ...

If advice has you feeling like you need to *fix* yourself in worrying ways you hadn't even thought of ...

If advice has you feeling 127 times more confused than ever ...

If advice has you heading under the doona and sobbing your heart out ...

You are normal.

In messy real life, things don't play out like they do on TV or in books. Those magical sparkling genies who really can help us make choices in difficult times and not feel worse are few and far between. Most of us regular humans are not really qualified or totally across every single aspect of our struggling person's life to give them truly informed ideas of 'where to next' or how to fix their situation.

Real human lives have all kinds of nuances, variables and challenges that mean the 'go-to' fix-it strategies very often *do not apply*.

It's okay to keep your inner circle small. It's okay to tell those closest to you that you can't cope with advice or opinions about your situation just yet. It's okay to let them know that their excellent big listening ears are about all you can cope with right now. And to tell them that having someone who is kind and present and able to sit and nod would be the very best thing as you put one foot in front of the other.

It's okay to simply say to them, 'I am feeling fragile. I just need someone to listen and be there, without giving me advice. I just need to unburden a bit and feel cared for — and not be judged or fixed.'

Okay. That's kinda long-winded, I'll admit, but you get the idea.

My point is, give yourself permission to *not take advice*.

It's okay to go through these tough feelings. You don't have to make them go away. They are there for a reason: to help you better understand your situation and yourself. The more you look at them, the less daunting they will be. Sooner or later you'll be able to go, 'Oh, there's that big hurt that's been lurking inside me, popping up again to make itself known. Must be time for a nap or a huge sob' or whatever else is helping you to pass through, as opposed to cast off, the feelings at hand.

If other people are trying to advice your feelings out of existence, the best thing to do is … forgive them and know that they care.

Know that, at the heart of it, there is someone keen to do anything to make you feel okay and help you get through this — and that you are strong enough and smart enough to also give *yourself* the advice you need, which will ultimately get you through this hard time.

Talking with the other humans

For me at least, dealing with a very hard time meant that I really needed to retreat into my own world. It felt like every new demand or contact outside my tiny circle/routine could catapult me into places I couldn't control.

It *felt* like the next phone call, email, knock at the door could tip things over irreparably. ('How will I manage it all? Will people notice I am freaking out? I am tired of these disasters! I am such a wreck, a broken person, and will be forever more ...') I would literally check my emails repeating the mantra, 'You can do this. You can deal with anything. Everything will be okay, eventually.'

This is probably not the case for everyone, but for me there was a hypervigilance that was hard to shake, an expectation of chaos or drama in the wake of sad events, which left me feeling constantly on edge, like I was about to be threatened or under attack.

When I spoke to my psychologist about this, she empathised and mentioned a book called *The Body Remembers* by Babette Rothschild, about how trauma affects — and is 'stored' by — the body and the brain.

We know that hypervigilance results in the release of the stress hormone cortisol, and makes us more prone to anxiety. We also know that the sort of prolonged stress characterised by hypervigilance affects the way our brains work. This means that things that we once found easy are temporarily not.

If this is you, note that your fear of people makes sense to your brain — and the rest of you — because of what's been going on, and that it's a protective sort of response. Your body is trying to help you.

I was watching a really highbrow show called *The Real Housewives of Cheshire* and one of the women had been going through a messy divorce. As she chatted to a fellow H-wife about her situation, she admitted that she couldn't do small talk during this period of upheaval, and I just sat right up and stared at the telly.

Not only was small talk very hard for me, even thinking about small talk or chatting in a relaxed manner made me seize up.

If this is you, it can help to know you're not a weirdo. It's something many people go through at some point.

Of course, not everyone is like me and wants to hide away when they are going through big difficult things. For many people, big difficult things do just the opposite, drawing them *towards* others. Acute social stress can increase the desire for closeness, something researchers refer to as tend-and-befriend behaviour.

Again, remember that it often helps to talk to your friends, especially if they're not sure what you're going through, and are wondering why you seem to have disappeared into a fort made of feelings and fluffy blankets.

Identify the trusty types who are worthy of your confidence. This might be a long-cherished best friend. A relative. A therapist.

People you should generally NOT confide in include:

a)
a gent at the bank

b)
a random person in a Facebook group

c)
anyone who has the words 'lifestyle guru' associated with their name!

24 NON-WRONG THINGS TO SAY
TO THE SAD PERSON IN YOUR LIFE

1. Can I help by doing X, Y or Z? Or is there something else I can do?

2. This is a temporary-yet-painful situation. It won't always be like this. And bloody hell, you are right, it DOES suck.

3. It IS hard to imagine a way out of this mess. We can think about where to start chipping away together after we eat these biscuits.

4. I'm here to listen whenever you need me. No matter when or why.

5. I'm so glad we're friends. Remember your X, Y and Z (insert character traits and strengths) are what brought us together? So pleased I met you.

6. I'm sorry you have to go through this. *Insert hug*

7. What are your thoughts on what's going on and why it's like this?

8. Sorry if I sometimes say stuff that shits you, but know that I'm here and I want to be the best pal I can be for you. Let me know if I stuff up so I can learn to do better.

9. It's so good to see you here. I know you've got a lot of stuff going on. So glad that the planets aligned today and we get to hang out.

10. Can I take you out for the day? For a drive? Get away from the usual and sip cold wine in a gastropub or some-such?

11. Can I take your pet/child/partner/housemate out for the day?

12. Here are some dumplings for you.

13. If you need someone to co-pilot with you at the GP, I'd be so happy to be that person.

14. I've made you something delicious. When can I leave it on your doorstep/kitchen table?

15. Can I come over and take you for a big walk? We can look at trees and stuff quietly, or we can talk … or not.

16. I can see you're trying your best. That's all you can do. Nice one.

17. I think this might be an *Uncle Buck/Ghostbusters/Young Ones*-and-hot-chips-and-G&T kind of day. What time should I bring all the laughs/carbs/booze over?

18. So today was a bit of a cock-up. Meh. It's okay to be messy. Forgive yourself and hope for a radder tomorrow.

19. You have a nap. I will tidy up and make dinner.

20. Can I assist you to find some more help with this? I think some extra support might offer a fresh perspective and maybe a little relief.

21. I'm not sure of the best way to help, but here is a bottle of Prosecco and some tissues. Where shall we sit?

22. It's not okay that you're having to endure this. I'm here to help in any way that makes sense to you. Let's start small. I wonder what small thing can we do to shift things a bit?

23. I'll call you again tomorrow to see how you're going. (Repeat daily.)

24. Yes. Sometimes pets *are* the most supportive people. So true.

Hugs might help

Look, some people *hate* hugs — but lots of people like them, especially during a hard time. And little wonder, because hugs actually have scientifically proven healing powers.

Turns out that hugs can reduce feelings of loneliness and anxiety, lower our blood pressure, and reduce levels of the stress hormone cortisol, which in turn helps strengthen our immunity.

Hugging also stimulates the production of our feel-good chemicals oxytocin, dopamine and serotonin. And one of the best ways to get your oxytocin flowing is by physical touch. Also, when oxytocin is released, it may also stimulate another chemical in our system called anandamide (nicknamed the 'bliss molecule'), which boosts feelings of happiness and wellbeing.

All the more reason to learn to like the hug. And seek it out, even.

Hugging for 20 seconds every morning with someone you care for reduces stress and readies us for the day, writes Zen Buddhist monk Haemin Sunim in his book, *Love for Imperfect Things*.

For people who have lost a person or pet from their life, hugs might be in very short supply. Those people might be longing for a hug … or at the very least a gentle touch or a bit of a hand hold.

Of course, restorative hugs from people you are close to can be hard to access at times. Note that hugs with nice animals provide many of the same benefits — so you're good go to with pet snuggles!

Luckily for me, I have a really tolerant dog who will let me hug and kiss him. If it weren't for him, I might have turned to stone during those hardest times.

Helpful info for friends and family of someone going through something tough

Struggling person, this is the section you casually leave open for your friends and family. It's full of simple, practical, concrete ideas on how they can help support you through your terrible times, when they might be feeling unsure of the best approach and are hand-wringingly anxious not to do the 'wrong' thing.

In fact, let them keep reading to the end of the chapter ...

HOW TO BE A GOOD LISTENER

In other words, how not to upset a person who is already upset enough, thank you very much ...

Say less ... aka SHOOSH!

Honestly, I know it's hard, but try not to talk too much. Just ask your sad person, 'Do you want to talk about it?' or 'Do you need to vent?' or 'How about you tell me all the crap stuff so I can get an idea of how you're going?'

Let them speak, and try not to interrupt them with your own thoughts and ideas.

Don't try to fix it

Noooo. Just don't. You might think trying to find a practical way to fix the problem is a helpful response, but often it can simply heighten a person's feelings of pain or hopelessness.

Once, when a friend of mine was having a really tough time, some well-meaning pals lovingly bombarded her with advice that included changing jobs, moving house, hiring a lawyer, seeking therapy and exposing her difficulties to family members. All in a space of about 35 minutes, at a time when she was struggling to get out of bed each day due to the trickiness of her situation.

While their intentions were wonderful, they accidentally pushed her further into anxiety and sadness as she pondered turning her currently rudderless life even further upside down.

Be an active listener

Active listening involves being fully present and focused on what the other person is saying.

Active listening isn't always easy. In fact, it can be really hard! However much you want to engage, you might drift off a tiny bit at times, random thoughts might pop into your head, you might be thinking of the next thing you want to say (try hard to stop that please), you might notice how uncomfy the position you are in is ... these are all normal.

That said, distracted listening can be unsettling for the person in pain who is trying to tell you their story. Please don't make them feel they don't matter by glazing over or fidgeting with the sugar bowl or repeatedly checking your phone.

If you're there to listen, do just that — and if you find yourself drifting, give yourself a little kick in the shins.

When someone in crisis very much needs to talk, pay close attention. Look them in the eye, and be patient.

Try to use open and encouraging body language and facial expressions, and nod or offer brief encouraging comments to show you are listening.

Avoid jumping in during pauses, and listen for cues that indicate feelings as well as details of what is happening with your person.

Respond carefully and compassionately. Rather than give advice, ask open-ended questions about what has been said — 'What's your gut telling you that you should do about this?' or 'Given what you've told me, what do you think might help you feel more secure?'

What to say (and what not to say) to your struggling person

People who are suffering from trauma don't need advice, say clinical psychologist Susan Silk and author Barry Goldman in a piece for the *Los Angeles Times* about how to support someone in crisis.

'They need comfort and support. So say, "I'm sorry" or "This must really be hard for you" or "Can I bring you a pot roast?"

'Don't say, "You should hear what happened to me!" or "Here's what I would do if I were you."

'And don't say, "This is really bringing me down."'

Empathy counts, but remember it's not about you

I am guilty of this, and I try so hard not to do it. What I want to get across to the suffering person is, 'I've been there, I understand' — but at times it can come out as, 'You're not so special, I've done that too. Let's talk a little bit about me, too.'

Err on the side of caution here, and if you catch yourself heading down the 'been there, done that' route, however well intentioned, turn back.

When your friend is in a better place, you might deign to share how their experience mirrored yours, but not right now. You could simply say to them, 'If you'd like to talk to someone who's been around the block, I am 153 per cent here for you.' No detail required, just a helpful offer.

Right now, it's all about understanding and having compassion for their feelings, and responding supportively and kindly. It's not about diminishing them with your own tough stuff.

Don't be an expert

Sometimes an 'expert' opinion, speedily delivered at someone's time of woe, may unintentionally waylay their recovery efforts, opening up a Pandora's box of further insecurity, simply because of the tone you use or the words you choose. You might even seem slightly dismissive or breezy as you survey their life and offer your lofty view of it.

Be a kind human seeking to connect and understand your pal's feelings — rather than dictating, analysing or summarising them.

Don't look for 'the gaps'

There's also something to be said for allowing some quiet spots in the conversation. Often, we try to fill silences, but when someone is talking about something difficult, giving them some space as they chat and process is important. Rather than cutting in, quietly look at them or nod or tilt your head to let them know that you are engaging with them.

Often, when we listen to someone, we're thinking backwards and forwards, trying to grasp the situation and how it has occurred — and what should happen next. Then we begin suggesting the things they haven't done, could do, should do.

Don't do this. Just don't. Not only does it make the person who is having a tough time feel anxious, it distances you from them. People going through hard times are very sensitive and on the lookout for signs and clues. They might see your gap-filling suggestions as a secret way for you to *not* get too involved. The gaps might also be providing some relief for your person, giving them a chance to reflect and take a breather, ideally with you by their side, not urging them to be more than they can be.

24 ways to help a struggling person

(JUST IN CASE YOU MISSED IT!)

1. Listen to your person (see 'How to be a good listener', page 127).

2. Do not judge your person.

3. Do not avoid your person.

4. Do not give your person unsolicited advice.

5. Do not tell them what is happening is God's will or similar.

6. Do not look for the silver lining in their situation. Definitely do not *tell* them there is a silver lining. If you do, they are allowed to poke you in the eye.

7. Don't make assumptions. Let them impart how they're feeling and what's going on for them when they are able or ready.

8. Don't be a know-all. Every crisis is nuanced.

9. Do not betray their confidence — close ranks and protect them.

10. Connect on their terms, not yours. They know what makes them feel best right now.

11. Be patient. Learning to cope with a big life change is incredibly difficult, so don't flake out on your friend — be in it for the long haul.

12. Be available when you can. Let them know you're there if they need to talk, even if they don't feel like it right now. Just being present for them when you can is what matters most. It might be very hard for them to make social contact. If they do, show up for them and be a good bud.

13. Understand that they are in a state of flux, and how they feel today may not be how they feel tomorrow.

14. Don't expect them to feel better each day — coping with grief, loss, trauma and difficulty is hard. It can be two steps forward and five steps back. Don't say things like, 'Are you feeling better?' or 'You seem so much better', as it can make your person feel like they must 'improve' to have your support.

15. Don't encourage them to make big life changes just yet. Let them do that in their own time.

16. Remember that small, thoughtful, simple things help a lot. Ask if there is something specific you can do to help them — like driving them to an appointment or taking them away for the weekend.

17. Stay in touch. Checking in *without* always asking 'How are you?' is super helpful. Even just send a nice 'hello' message or a card or flowers or dumplings to let them know you're thinking of them.

18. Don't stop inviting them to things. Include them without making them feel obliged. You could say, 'I wanted to ask you for lunch. I'm going to ask X and Y too. I will understand if you don't feel up to it. You don't need to explain and I love you no matter what. But if you'd like to come you are so welcome.'

19. Don't drift away or ghost them. No matter how many times they are unable to be part of your plans, don't stop including them. They are not rejecting you. They are doing what they need to survive.

20. Support them through 'big days' — anniversaries or birthdays or other special events that are hard to endure when things are tough.

21. If your person is active on social media, don't assume things are as they seem — social media makes life look way peachier than it is. They may be lonely and feeling horrendous. Check in and let them know that they can talk to you or simply spend time with you.

22. And speaking of social media, don't assume the odd social media message from you has them covered. Social media is a very noisy but lonely platform and it's *really* not the same as making real-life contact.

23. Look after yourself — if you are helping someone through a crisis, make sure that you support your own mental and physical health, too.

24. Encourage your person to ask for the help they need — from you or others. (See 'How can you help someone get professional help?' on page 138.)

Don't leave them hanging

If you've been listening to your sad person as they unload about the challenges they are going through, don't simply soak it all up and walk away. Your friend will feel a bit bewildered ... as though they've revealed their big things and you've just abandoned them in favour of your own generally busy and interesting life.

Offer them a reassuring hand squeeze. Suggest another catch up, such as a walk and talk around the park. A roam about the bookshop next to the cafe you were in, where you buy them a really fetching bookmark and remind them that you are there for them, no matter what. A quick duck into a dumpling joint for 42 shared parcels of saucy, vinegary mystery.

Keep checking in with them and let them know it wasn't a one-off, and that you're there should they need you. (And even when they can't manage to tell you they need you.) Message them: 'Just wanted to say hello! Love to you!' Or call them: 'Just wanted to hear your voice. Thinking of you today!'

You don't need to get into the feelings stuff when you check in, because the timing might not be right, but just flagging that you're around and your pal is in your thoughts counts for a lot, and shows them that they matter.

Remember, try not to judge

- It's so easy to *think* you know how you would deal with things if you were in a sad and similar situation ... but truth be told, life rolls out so very differently for each of us. Folks. Strokes. Your way is not the highway.

- Your friend has to find their own way through, and letting them do that — with some ever-loving, rock-solid support from you — is a sensible approach.

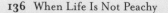

How your friendship can help your friend heal

Helping someone through their hardest times, on their own terms, in ways that make sense to them, is a huge opportunity to build a deeper friendship. And the things you learn from diving deep have a knock-on effect in your other relationships.

And please don't think that old friends are the only ones that make a difference. Friends that show up and empathise — or have been through or are going through something similar — can make a huge difference.

Rest assured that just by being a good friend, by being there for your person, you are helping them to recover.

Again, it's also super-important to care for your own mental health as you help someone else, but note that allowing yourself to have a real and deep friendship with another human comes with its own health benefits for both buddies. It's a wellbeing-promoting, protective, heart-softening and generally transformative experience.

Finding a balance between providing support and establishing your own health-promoting boundaries is key here. It's not an easy one, but it comes down to being mindful of how you are managing your role as your friend's helper, and finding your own support crew if you're struggling a bit with looking after yourself and caring about your buddy, so you don't end up feeling resentful.

It's worth the juggle though, because these close friendships can provide a sort of baseline for our life — something steady to hang on to as we begin to move ahead.

Increasingly, social media and modern life in general might conspire to make our friendships a little more surface-level. Social media places an emphasis on the *quantity* of friends and interactions, rather than the *quality* of our friendships. That's not to say it's all bad, but it can leave people looking very popular, yet feeling very lonely. [*Coughs*]

So here's your chance to go *big* and go *in*.

Be there for your friend in authentic, messy, real ways that count.

Be a quality friend.

How can you help someone get professional help?

Sometimes, somebody you care about might be really deep in their tough time and may not be able to put their hand up for help. They may not feel comfortable doing so, or may not realise how intolerable things are getting.

The longer someone navigates a difficult situation, the longer it can take for them to recover, so facilitating the right support can help your person feel better sooner.

From my own experience, I know that I needed to arrive at finding professional support in my own way, and in my own time. That said … I took too long! I didn't realise how much relief it would offer. Quite the opposite: I thought that having to talk about all my issues would make me fall apart! It didn't. I simply had no idea how non-threatening seeing a therapist could be, and that it would become a partnership for my greater good. Which it was.

But how do you go about broaching this delicate situation?

First, make sure you are the right person for the job. Is there somebody closer to your person who might be in a more appropriate position to help? Note that this support person will probably have some misgivings about raising the issue with them, so you could help by pointing them to Chapter 10, which explains a little more about what happens when a person accesses professional support.

Do your research. Find out what services your person might be able to access. Consider their financial situation as you make enquiries.

Choose your moment. Don't just blurt it out. Find a quiet time when your person is not under pressure or distracted.

Think about what you'd like to say. You could try something like: 'I can see you're finding this hard time really challenging. And understandably so. Would you like me to help you find someone who can offer some extra support? I am happy to come with you, if you feel worried about doing that.'

Listen carefully and actively to their response (I mentioned some tips for that on page 128).

Try not to be judgemental or feel disappointed that they are 'not doing enough' to help themselves.

Remember, listen but don't advise

Oh, but this is so hard, right? But really, it's the best way. Struggling pal may be sad, but they need to come to their own grown-up decisions about their life, when the time is right for them. Listen carefully and let them know you care about how they're feeling and that you're there, no matter what. The rest is up to them.

You can most definitely help them enlist the assistance of a professional person to guide them through, but don't take on the role of doctor or counsellor or therapist yourself. Some things are best supported by the professionals — but you can co-support, right? Yep.

If they say no, tell them you understand, and that if they change their mind you're ready to spring into action.

Keep the dialogue open. Look at other ways to help them access information that may assist them — such as books or podcasts, for instance. Try again another time.

Keep supporting them. Try not to be judgemental or feel disappointed that they're 'not doing enough' to help themselves. Instead, accept their response at this time and continue to stand by them, so that they don't feel isolated, alone or rejected.

I'm reminded here of a passage from E.B. White's classic children's tale, *Charlotte's Web*, where Wilbur the pig asks Charlotte, 'Why did you do all this for me? I don't deserve it. I've never done anything for you.'

Charlotte simply replies, 'You have been my friend. That in itself is a tremendous thing.'

CHAPTER 7

A 'IOI' for looking after yourself

In our society,
we can be a little
too obsessed
with moving
on and feeling
better.

WE'RE URGED TO brush aside things that make us feel terrible. Phrases like 'First World problem' are thrown about. We're urged to suck it up or check our privilege or put our big girl pants on.

'There are many worse off than you,' some tough-loving types will tell us. And very often that is true. But someone else's pain doesn't magic away our own. A dose of perspective doesn't erase suffering. Fact is, when something awful happens, it takes time to process it.

You don't have to cheer up, get it together, snap out of it or be anything other than the way you currently need to be.

Take that time and know that *you* will know when it's time to shift or pivot a little.

Self-care during a crisis is a very personal thing, but here are some ideas to crack on with — some ways you might help look after *you*, when you feel good and ready.

Take a leaf out of
Bryony's book and
choose one each
morning …

How do you feel today?

Artist Bryony Kimmings once spoke on a
BBC Radio I *Life Hacks* podcast about how she
navigated post-traumatic stress disorder after
her little boy had a health crisis.

She said one truly helpful thing she does
each day is stand in front of the mirror and
ask herself how she's feeling. This prompts
a moment of self-reflection and also sparks
a self-care plan for that particular day.

Hearing this, I realised I wish I'd asked
myself that question my whole life: 'How do
you actually feel today?'

I feel really delicate today.

'Then take care of yourself. Don't go
and have a stressful day. You feel vulnerable,
so don't beat yourself up all day.'

So, what are some of those feelings? I've
made a list for your choosing pleasure. Take
a leaf out of Bryony's book and choose one
each morning …

Be kind to you

When we judge ourselves and our response to a
crisis, we tend to be pretty black and white. We
hear the perceived or real voices of others in
our heads, and we turn those on ourselves.

How do I really feel
this morning?

- hopeful
- self-conscious
- insecure
- unsure
- shy
- introverted
- happy
- joyful
- pleased
- delighted
- carefree
- buoyant
- jealous
- protective
- melancholy
- vigilant
- optimistic
- confident

- positive
- loving
- tender
- warm
- mad
- suspicious
- cynical
- sceptical
- dubious
- lonely
- sad
- devastated
- neglected
- abandoned
- sorrowful
- depressed
- miserable
- heartbroken

- hurt
- angry
- frustrated
- annoyed
- irritated
- furious
- threatened
- scared
- frightened
- nervous
- resentful
- panicky
- intimidated
- alarmed
- anxious
- startled
- unsafe
- affectionate

I think, conversationally, society can be pretty simplistic about life — encouraging us to do things like buck up, blame ourselves, be accountable. To beat ourselves up when things go wrong ... to assume we're not doing a good enough job of coping.

But in reality, life can be complicated — and *we* can be complicated. It's important to make room for nuanced responses to big changes and sad things.

Often, we have good reason for behaving in certain ways. Generally, there's no 'right' way to respond, and everyone is different. But some of the time we are pretty much the same.

One brilliant benefit I've found from going to a psychologist is that she points out where I'm making assumptions about myself that are not really based on reality. For instance, I might assume I'm incapable of forming strong bonds with any new people. That I can't be trusted to judge character wisely and might get myself involved with people who want to take advantage of me.

She'll point out that I actually have a wealth of experience, that I'm primed for red flags, that I can draw my own line in the sand ...

Where I might say, 'What if this is a pattern?', she responds with, 'But you learned something — and you know more now.'

Very often, we are dealing with things the best we can — willing ourselves forward at an appropriate speed, however slowly.

It is — as my psych says — a form of convalescence.

One of the biggest and best acts of self-care is to allow yourself time to convalesce, and to put in place the support systems and strategies that help most during this recovery period.

A bit about hygiene and grooming

Ugggggghhhh. This is a toughie because it's not something we talk about a lot ... I feel embarrassed just typing this.

The thing is, however, hygiene and grooming can fall by the wayside when you are feeling at your worst. And this can then make you feel even worse — about yourself, life, the universe ... everything.

Often it's simply due to a lack of energy. Perhaps it's a sneaky way to punish ourselves.

GENERAL TIDY HUMAN STUFF THAT MIGHT FALL OUT OF YOUR DAILY GROOMING AND SELF-CARE ROUTINES DUE TO EXHAUSTION, SADNESS OR APATHY INCLUDE:

- Bathing regularly — perhaps in favour of falling into bed or rushing off to work late again.

- Looking after your hair — washing, brushing, cutting.

- Looking after your teeth — brushing, flossing, dental visits.

- Looking after your skin — which is probably feeling very lacklustre.

- General health maintenance — avoiding the doctor because you feel vulnerable.

- Sleeping properly — treating the night as you would the day, due to insomnia or sleep problems.

- Eating properly — forgoing good nutrition because you're too tired to care about what you put into your body.

- Abusing alcohol and recreational drugs — using these in ways that your less-distressed self would probably not.

I'm not going to tell you which ones on this list affected me — but at various hellish times, some of them did. And you know what? Further research confirmed that these are 'normal' things that happen to even the most brilliant humans during 'not normal' times.

How can simple things be so hard? Well they just can, that's how.

Please, please, please don't judge yourself harshly if you've been in this place. Also please don't see this as confirmation that you suck and somehow deserve this horrible time. If this has happened to you or is happening to you, rest assured you are in good company. It's not a sign of terrible character or hopeless human-ing.

Instead, it's a sign that you are navigating a shitty time in the best way you can — a little bit the worse for wear, admittedly. Know that your clever brain is trying to preserve as much energy as possible so that you may retreat, process, convalesce, fortify yourself and slowly re-emerge when you're ready.

Here's a small tip for navigating these untidy times. Set an alarm on your phone to remind you to do the most pressing looking-after-yourself task — and try to make it non-negotiable if you can. Make sure it's at a time that's practical — like just after you get up, or just before you go to bed. You'll feel a wee boost once you've done the thing and it'll feel like progress, even if it is simply combing-the-knots-out-of-your-messy-hair progress.

And if you sometimes skip it because you can't even contemplate doing anything except breathing, remember that tomorrow's another day. Don't waste your precious time berating yourself over it. Just move on.

Quick fist bump to the 'tidy' sufferers, too!

My friend Michelle Mackintosh happens to be an expert on Japanese bath houses. Over the page she kindly explains how to create a beautifully relaxing and purifying bathing ritual at home.

DIY bath fix

My naturopath friend Gill Stannard has a simple, restorative bath remedy for soothing stressed-out souls.

- Her favourite DIY bath fix is an oat bag infused with fresh or dried herbs. Put a tablespoon or two of rolled oats in a square of muslin, or a clean hanky or stocking. Add a big handful of fresh herbs such as lavender or lemon balm, or a small handful of dried herbs or dried chamomile flowers. Tie up the bag and throw it into the bath as you run the water. The oats are full of saponin, a soap-like constituent that makes a gentle alternative to soap to suds your body, while the herbs have relaxing medicinal qualities.

- You can also make a pot of strong relaxing tea to add to the bath, using fragrant relaxing herbs such as lavender and chamomile. Let it steep in the teapot for 5 minutes or so first. (Gill uses herbal tea in a bath to administer herbs to babies, through the skin and inhalation; sometimes we forget how good it is for adults as well!)

- For added benefits, throw a cupful or two of epsom salts into the bath. They're full of muscle-relaxing magnesium.

- To de-stress, Gill loves walking, gardening (or even admiring other people's gardens), cuddles with cats, frolicking with dogs, journalling, the smell of the lemon-scented gum trees after the rain, walking barefoot on grass or sand, observing the moon through its phases, looking at the stars, drinking pots of herbal tea, listening to music, dancing and …

Bathing through tough times: a Japanese onsen at home

by Michelle Mackintosh, co-author of *Onsen of Japan*

I think we have all used bathing to soak away stress, soothe sore limbs and generally relax. I love to have a bath on a Sunday when I have a bit of time to myself and can soak away the afternoon.

In a Japanese onsen, or hot spring bath, you first take a really good shower or scrub so you are clean and pristine before you enter the bath, which is often communal, and can be indoors or outdoors, with an arresting view of nature.

Everyone is there to soak and unwind, so the mood can be chatty and infectiously happy, or quiet and peaceful. I like to find a cosy spot, shut my eyes, and feel the steamy water swirl around me, clearing my mind and centering my thoughts.

When you discard your clothes and daily cares, you enter the bath with an open heart and mind. In Japan, even though I didn't speak the language, through simple, 'naked' communication I have been invited to dinner and to stay at people's houses, had my back scrubbed and been given food and small trinkets.

Every time I have an onsen I feel deeply relaxed, I sleep better, and have more energy the next day.

What you'll need

- A fresh towel.

- A jug of cold water or cold green tea, and your favourite teacup.

- A small clothes basket.

- Japanese bath salts (available online or from Japanese grocery stores), or make your own by combining epsom salts, essential oils or green tea.

- Candles or music (optional).

What to do

- Make sure your bathroom is pristinely clean.

- Turn your phone off.

- Run a hot bath — as hot as you can manage.

- Light candles and turn on music if you like; silence and darkness are also really lovely.

- Place the cold water or tea within arm's reach.

- Undress, then fold your clothes and place them neatly in the basket.

- Submerge as deeply as you can, and close your eyes.

- Lie perfectly still. Utterly relax. Meditate.

- Do some yoga breathing: inhale a positive word like 'relax' or 'peace' or 'calm', then exhale a negative word like 'stress' or 'sadness'.

- Stay in the bath as long as you possibly can, sipping tea and yoga breathing.

- Just before you get out, wash yourself. This bath is not about getting clean, so if you haven't already had a shower that day, use the last part of the bath to de-grime.

- Get cosy in your fluffy towel, put your nicely folded clothes back on — and just like that, you've reset your mind for the rest of the day!

Sleep, wellbeing and memory

Never feel bad about prioritising sleep, because it is a vital restorative for those of us who have been through the wringer.

Sleep is essential for good mental health, with REM ('rapid eye movement') sleep in particular playing a core role. It appears that as we sleep, our brains are busily processing and integrating the day's experiences and helping us to modulate our feelings and mood.

Research tells us that many adults with major depression, generalised anxiety disorder or post-traumatic stress disorder experience some kind of sleep problem. Most patients with depression have insomnia, and around one in five suffer from sleep apnoea.

Sleep problems increase the risk of depression, increase the chance of mental health relapses, and can also interfere with antidepressant medication.

Sleeplessness or insomnia can also make anxiety symptoms more acute. And people who suffer from insomnia have double the risk of developing an anxiety disorder.

Sleep as a healing tonic

When you are battling with sleep deprivation, your memory and cognitive abilities take a hit. So if you have been feeling vague or forgetful or even clumsy, it's not a sign of dorkiness — it's actually your body responding to your sleep debt.

It kind of fits with the way people under pressure, who are sleeping less and less, are also finding that they are remembering less and less, and buggering things up more and more.

Once I realised that my own memory was being affected by things other than ... my own stupidity ... I set about moving on from surviving in those early days and weeks (and months) by paying more attention to sleep hygiene.

It felt pretty great to stop blaming my memory issues on what I saw as my 'failing self'. Being able to sleep a little more normally made me feel that better days were ahead.

Which fits with what the science is telling us. Studies have found that the human brain is naturally more attentive to negative events, and that when we are sleep-deprived, our brains are less likely to respond to positive stimuli, and we are more likely to have greater anxiety levels, because those parts of the brain that regulate emotions are very sensitive to sleep loss.

Okay, great. Now we feel anxious about feeling anxious — and anxious about sleep. Sigh.

Perhaps it will make you feel a little better to know that once we get a decent night's sleep, the parts of the brain that regulate emotion work optimally once more. When we are well rested, so are the regions of the brain that help keep us calm and much less anxious.

So how *can* the wakeful get a bit more shut-eye, especially when there are lots of things weighing heavy on their minds?

How to promote sleep — according to science

Professor Matthew Walker, the director of UC Berkeley's Sleep and Neuroimaging Lab, is the author of a book called *Why We Sleep: Unlocking the Power of Sleep and Dreams*, and he has heaps of ideas about how to promote sleep. A lot of them are super simple to implement.

LIGHTS OUT!

We are dark-deprived in our modern world and it's messing with our bodies. I wrote more about sleep and the benefits of sleeping under the stars and its cycle-resetting benefits in my book *Craft For the Soul*.

At night, Professor Walker recommends turning off as many lights as possible, and dimming them if you can. Also, avoid screens before bedtime, which leads us to the following ...

AVOID SCREENS

The screens on our laptops and mobile phones block the sleep-inducing hormone melatonin, Professor Walker tells us, by a whopping 60 per cent, and delays your melatonin spike by around 3 hours. Vital REM sleep is also reduced.

In the hours before you go to bed, reduce exposure to blue light, which is emitted by electronic devices and low-energy light bulbs.

HIT THE RIGHT TEMPERATURE

The right temperature is just as important as light when it comes to getting a good night's sleep, because your brain has to drop its core temperature by a few degrees to fall asleep. Professor Walker suggests keeping your room coolish — at around 18°C, or 65°F.

Warming up other parts of your body can help you sleep better. In winter, wearing socks or putting a hot water bottle in the bed can help you drift off.

Another good trick is to have a warm bath. When you get out, the blood races to the surface of your skin, away from your core — and brain — and you lose heat, so your body temperature dips, helping you sleep more easily.

NAP WISELY

You want to build up what Professor Walker calls 'sleep pressure', and he says that having a nap can relieve some of the pressure you really need to sleep well all night. That's not to say naps are out, but if you're having issues with sleeping through the night, he suggests avoiding naps until things are on a more even keel.

We actually seem to be programmed to take a nap in the afternoon, but if you want to know more about how long you should nap for and the benefits of different types of naps ... you gotta buy Professor Walker's book! Obviously I don't want to spill all his best stuff here since he's the genius that did all the hard work.

EXPERTS ALSO TELL US ...

Sleep regularity is important.	Banish booze.	Avoid caffeine.
Go to bed at the same time and wake up at the same time every day, even on weekends. And if you can't sleep, get up. If you stay in bed, your brain learns that bed does not equal sleep.	Alcohol has sedating properties, but doesn't actually help you sleep. In fact, it results in fragmented sleep, even if you don't realise it, and you'll feel utterly exhausted when you get up in the morning.	Caffeine will block your body's sleepy signals for more than 12 hours, so it's best to avoid it 12–14 hours before you plan to go to bed.

10 SCIENCE-BACKED SLEEP-INDUCING STEPS

Here's a quick summary of what I know, from my my own personal experience and research.

1. Avoid consuming caffeine and chocolate after 1 pm.

2. If it's warm, cool your room down just before bed time.

3. Make sure you have lunch. And dinner, but not too close to bedtime.

4. Make your bed nicely, to make it feel inviting.

5. Have a long, hot shower. Or a bath.

6. Turn all the lights off — block out any light sources (except your reading light).

7. Check for annoying noises. Stop them if you can.

8. Hop into bed — without your digital devices. So, no checking social media or emails in bed!

9. Read a calming book or listen to soothing music until you feel sleepy …

10. … and fall asleep …

A bit about drinking during tough times

Perhaps you are careering through your days with the promise of a gin and tonic or three or a bottle of wine to get you through? The temptation to sip your way to a less upset state is very understandable, but what you might end up doing is drinking too much to numb things away.

I thought it would be good to talk about this, so you can determine if this is really doing you any favours. You will know what is best for you.

I tried having a glass of wine or three at the end of the day, and also avoiding alcohol altogether, in a quest to find some 'peace'. So what did I find out?

In the end, I decided avoiding alcohol is best for me. When I wound down with wine at the end of the day (and I'm talking just a couple of glasses, generally), it just took me to different place. It was a sort of respite in that it paused and shifted life a little.

But I felt terrible when I woke up. I felt like I had been diverted from myself, and even lost myself, and I always wondered why I even bothered. Perhaps it was due to my own hang-ups (I have family members with addiction issues), but I found drinking only added to my confusion, and ultimately to my sadness.

There is so much pressure and culture around drinking, and that's fine — but it's not actually what is best for everyone, especially if you are feeling pretty fragile and unsure of yourself.

With the benefit of hindsight, I found that not drinking when I was toughing things out kept me feeling clearer, conscious and more in control. It didn't add a pile of extra worries — like how I behaved when I was drinking, or how I felt when waking up, or the physical damage alcohol might be doing to my already beleaguered body.

It also helped me feel good about myself, knowing I was doing something excellent for my mental and physical health.

But please don't think I would ever judge you if *not* drinking is too hard at the moment. You do you.

It's just that sometimes, hearing someone else's experience can help you understand your own. So I am sharing mine in case you've been struggling with the ubiquitous 'wine time' and its aftermath.

Also? That's not to say that I don't drink at all. But I know that falling into a pattern of using alcohol to wind down and feel some relief does not work for me — and in fact makes me feel worse about most things.

If you are finding that you are drinking more than you'd like, or that it is affecting your life in ways that you're not happy about, there are plenty of good folk who can help you work through this and decide the best next steps for you.

(Just Google 'em!)

And if other things — drugs, food, risky or harmful behaviours — are becoming a coping mechanism, head to your GP. It's really hard to heal yourself all by yourself.

Some helpful apps and websites to help reduce your alcohol intake include ...

•

Hello Sunday Morning

•

Soberistas

•

I Am Sober

•

Saying When

•

Drinkaware

•

Rethinking Drinking

10 sleep-boosting bedtime drinks

1. **Cherry juice**: Tart cherry juice helps boost sleep-inducing melatonin levels. If you can't find it at your local supermarket, try a Turkish or European grocer.

2. **Blueberry juice**: Blueberries are rich in procyanidins and anthocyanins, and have anti-inflammatory properties that can help with sleep.

3. **Soy, almond butter and banana smoothie**: These ingredients are all rich in sleep-promoting magnesium.

4. **A warm cup of bone broth**: Look … in my day we called this stock, but who am I to argue with a rich sip that promises to soothe and calm nerves without a wakeful hit?

5. **Milk**: If you like milk, this is an easy one! Warm or cold, it contains L-tryptophan, an amino acid that induces sleep.

6. **Chamomile tea**: Good old chamomile tea relaxes nerves and muscles, working a bit like a mild tranquilliser.

7. **Lavender tea**: I like my lavender in the bath, but it also has sleep-inducing properties if you make tea from it.

8. **Decaffeinated green tea**: Regular green tea is lovely, but it will not help you sleep due to its caffeine content, so go for the decaf variety.

9. **Lemon balm tea**: Grow your own lemon balm to make a soothing cup of snoozy tea each night.

10. **Sleepy teas**: There are heaps of 'sleep tea' blends available these days. Check out your local health food shop or supermarket.

Plants that help you sleep

If you are keen to buy a leafy pal to help you optimise your sleep environment, these guys are a good place to start.

Peace lily
Peace lilies (*Spathiphyllum*) appear to remove toxins from the air, while also releasing moisture into the air. They thrive in shady and semi-shady, places making them the perfect bedside bud.

Valerian
While experts remain divided on whether valerian is really helpful when taken orally, it has been found that people who breathe in the plant's scent do sleep more soundly, and for longer. Have a sniff of it?

Lavender
This fragrant plant is well-known for its sleep-inducing qualities. You could add some drops of lavender essential oil to your bath, or simply grow your own.

Snake plant
Sansevieria, also known as devil's tongue, bow string hemp, snake tongue and mother-in-law's tongue, is robust and purifies the air in a room. NASA tested this champion plant and found it removes at least 107 known air pollutants. Sleep easy in your clean-aired room, dear reader.

Bamboo palm
This palm (*Chamaedorea*) purifies the air and is also a natural humidifier, producing one litre of ambient water every 24 hours, which is brilliant news if you live in a very dry climate.

Self-care — tuning in to what helps

In this chapter, I didn't want to talk about how to *not feel terrible*, but rather how to break the 'survival' cycle and find some new — albeit wobbly — ways to be, so that at least *some* of the time you are feeling a bit more prepared to tackle the things that everyday life brings.

You start small and, however begrudgingly, notice the things that do feel good and comforting and safe.

It's a slippery slope from feeling the thing that is happening to you is shite, to feeling the entire world and indeed life in general is shite. So, at a time when it feels like we have so very little worth liking, let's think about what we *do* have.

Here are some ideas that will *definitely* help you to look after yourself a little better and create some fresh, new and even hopeful patterns for your new and different life.

'Closed caption' mindfulness

During some particularly dark days, I discovered the benefits of Korean reality TV.

As great as Korean TV is — shout-out to *Hyori's Bed and Breakfast* — it was actually the fact that I could not understand a word of it that made me feel a whole lot better. I had to turn on closed captions, and when I read along, it shut out everything else that was making life so hard. For the time it took for an episode to play out, at least.

I was used to multi-tasking and clogging up my brain with lots of taxing simultaneous processes. This just made me feel even more overwhelmed and confused.

The simple act of stopping all that bonkers activity and concentrating on one — wholesome — thing helped immensely. It was like a little brain holiday and provided some respite from everything else that was going on.

Of course, you don't have to stick to Korean television to feel the benefits of this. You could watch French films or Japanese game shows or Spanish soap operas, even?

Yesssss!

Wobbly (but good) new routines

Back in the 1970s, British psychiatrist Colin Murray Parkes wrote about the weird feeling of searching and yearning that happens when we suffer a loss or big shift. Parkes described this feeling as a kind of 'restlessness', and I think he's onto something.

And while processing and feeling our way through this state is important, it gets to a point where you don't want to feel this way anymore. Plugging up the gaps with some new things can help, even if you have to force yourself to crack on as you find your new 'normal'.

Usual everyday routines can provide a comforting framework as you strive to feel better and push on. But they can also prove a little challenging when times are tough: often we notice the shifts in those routines, which can make things feel super-sad and difficult.

For me, many familiar routines made me more aware of how things in my life had changed, and it was really pretty painful. But other trusty processes — like work, for instance — made me feel like I knew what I was doing and things would be okay after all.

When your days are full, things can seem slightly more bearable. Often, the more unscheduled moments can be the hardest — those quieter times at the end of the day or on the weekends, when the quiet can seem very shouty and you might feel the pull of heartache or pesky daggers of despair.

You will, of course, have your own responses as you go about your days. These are hard times, chickens. And they pop up again and again. This is where having some go-to new routines can help.

Things to do in those new and restless moments

Some of these ideas may sound revoltingly chipper if you're very deep in a dark time. But honestly, at some point you may realise that those activity-free or solo gaps in your days are really hard to handle.

Here are some things to edge toward when that happens. You'll find lots more ideas for helpful new habits in Chapter 11.

- Phone a friend and have a proper long chat.

- Buy a classic book you haven't read and turn to it when things are especially empty or glum.

- Write a letter to a beloved family member.

- Work your way through a bucket list of vintage films.

- Start collecting and listening to old CDs.

- Start a 'progress practice' that can be your go-to for moments when you are stuck (see Chapter 11).

- Spend time with a pet/ get a pet.

- Start learning how to play an instrument.

- Take an online course.

- Cook your way through a classic recipe book.

Try a little kindness

At a time when you want most want people to be kind to you, turning that kindness outward and finding ways to care for others can help to ease your own pain, literally.

When humans do good, we experience something called a 'helper's high', due to the release of the neurotransmitters dopamine and serotonin in our brains.

Doing something nice also strengthens the bonds you have with the other humans in your community — and makes you feel a little better about yourself and people in the process.

Kindness is also contagious: the more you practise it, the more you want to. And the people on the receiving end will often catch the kindness bug, too.

Obviously, when we are having a rough time ourselves, it can be hard to reach out and help others, but you could — once again — start small. It might be something as simple as writing a note and dropping it in a stranger's letterbox: 'I just wanted to thank you for your beautiful garden. I've been having a rough time but when I drive past and see all your flowers it makes me feel happier.'

Or letting someone cut in line ahead of you.

Or patting a cat you don't know.

You get the picture, I'm sure. Remember you can also do things for people you know, and for yourself.

Kindness is not just for strangers, obviously.

Helpful, hopeful to-dos

1. Leave a bunch of hand-picked flowers for a favourite person, or on the bus for a stranger, even!

2. Sneak a handwritten quote into a book at your favourite bookshop.

3. Find out if there is a meal sharing program in your local area, and cook a meal for an elderly or housebound person.

4. Bring your neighbour's bin in — even just pop it inside their front gate — when you do your own. I would LOVE this. I hate bringing the bins in!

5. Volunteer at your local library's home library service, and drop off books to folk who can't get out and about.

6. Slow things down to make space for others in a sort of everyday kindness pledge — make room for cars that want to merge, don't race for that parking space or taxi.

CHAPTER 8

How to feed yourself

FOOD IS A very good thing because it keeps us alive and it has the power to make us feel good.

Still, I am going to tell you what you already know: that eating well can help you feel a bit more okay as you push through hard days.

This is not just a thing that mums say. Science tells us that the right kinds of foods can improve not only physical but mental health, whereas eating really crap food can lead to a whole host of ills such as inflammation, brain chemistry irregularities and problems in the gut. And that's just for starters.

In particular, a traditional Mediterranean diet has been found to be associated with reduced risk of depressive symptoms, while also promoting general good health and wellbeing. It's a favourite of nutrition gurus such as Dr Michael Mosley, and has been enjoyed by clever Italian people for millennia, so who are we to argue?

A group of researchers at the Food and Mood Centre at Deakin University agree that diet can play a very important part in mood, and are focusing on diet and nutrition as a way to help prevent and treat mental ill health.

The researchers are also developing an app called 'My Food and Mood' to help people track their diet and how it affects their mood. Sounds super-helpful to me.

When you are in a tough spot you might ...

a)
Not feel like eating.

b)
Be too tired to cook.

c)
Want to eat everything to the point of not feeling good.

d)
Buy things to eat and then not want them anymore.

e)
Buy things to eat and then forget to eat them.

f)
Forget to buy anything.

g)
Do a mixture of the above.

Food really does affect mood

The Food and Mood Centre is headed by Professor Felice Jacka, a highly qualified scientist who is also president of the International Society for Nutritional Psychiatry Research. In her brilliant book *Brain Changer: The Good Mental Health Diet*, Professor Jacka describes her own experience of depression as feeling like she'd been 'attacked by a dementor from the Harry Potter books'.

Professor Jacka has been studying the relationship between diet and mental health for years, and wrote her book in a quest to help her fellow humans reduce their risk of depression and anxiety through good nutrition. For optimal wellbeing, she recommends a diet based on wholesome, simple unprocessed foods.

And there is good evidence for this. One study of 10,000 people found that people living on a traditional Mediterranean diet — with lots of vegetables, wholegrains, legumes, nuts, fruit, olive oil and fish, and not much red meat — were about *half as likely* to develop depression than those who ate less healthy food.

It is recommended that people with post-traumatic stress disorder:

1
Follow a 'traditional' dietary pattern, like the Mediterranean, Norwegian or Japanese diet (see opposite).

2
Eat more fruits, vegetables, legumes, wholegrains, nuts and seeds.

3
Avoid ultra-processed foods.

4
Choose wholesome nutritious foods for every meal and snack.

Some loose global 'better' mood food guidelines

Nordic feel-good eating

Plenty of: Fruits, berries, vegetables, legumes, potatoes, wholegrains, nuts, seeds, rye bread, fish, seafood, low-fat dairy, herbs, spices and canola oil

A bit of: game meats, free-range eggs, cheese and yoghurt

Very little of: other red meats and animal fats, sweets

Mediterranean feel-good eating

Plenty of: vegies, grains (mostly whole), fruit, olive oil, beans, nuts, seeds, legumes, herbs and spices

Some: fish/seafood

A bit of: chicken, eggs and dairy

A little: meats and sweets

Japanese feel-good eating

Plenty of: grains, vegetables, legumes, nuts and seeds

Some: meat and fish

A bit of: fruit and dairy

A little: sweets

A Mediterranean diet is also associated with a lower incidence of heart disease, cancer, Parkinson's disease and Alzheimer's disease, according to the respected Mayo Clinic.

Another study in nearly 3500 British public servants found those who ate diets high in fat, sugar and processed foods were around 60 per cent more likely to develop depression — with sweetened desserts, fried foods, processed meats, refined grains and high-fat dairy products being particularly flagged as depression-sparking foods.

Professor Jacka's own team studied 1000 Australian volunteers and found the very same thing — a 'traditional' diet (characterised by vegetables, fruits, meat, fish and wholegrains) reduced the incidence of depressive and anxiety disorders, whereas a 'Western' diet (processed and fried foods, refined grains, sugary products and beer) was associated with an increased rate of depression and anxiety.

Definitely food for thought if you're feeling lacklustre, or the dementors are sucking the joy out of you. Science is increasingly showing us that feeding up on the good stuff really can help improve our mental and physical wellbeing.

A gut feeling

We also now know that diet affects the balance of bacteria in our gut, which in turn affects our mental health. Incredible, I know. It's an evolving field, but lots of research is being done to see what exactly is going on in our gut, and what this all means for our overall wellbeing.

In short, watch this space, because this stuff is all super-promising.

For instance, a Belgian study in just over 1000 people, published in early 2019, found that two sorts of microbes were missing in those who were suffering from depression — but the same two microbes were present in those who didn't have depression. They then looked at another 1064 Dutch people, and found the same thing: those same two microbes were also missing in the depressed people among that second group, including seven people with severe clinical depression.

Professor Jacka explains in her book *Brain Changer* that there's constant communication between the brain and the gut, via what's known as the gut–brain axis. This means what's going on in our head is having a big impact on the bugs that live in our gut, and how quickly our food is digested. This in turn affects our immune system, metabolism, brain health, stress-response system, brain plasticity and more.

While it's not fully clear how these findings might affect the future treatment of depression, the research seems to show that these gut microbes also affect the production of neurotransmitters — such as serotonin and dopamine — that are crucial for good mental health.

'More than 90 *per cent* of our serotonin is produced in the gut,' Professor Jacka points out in her book *Brain Changer*. (My italics, not hers.)

Professor Jacka also explains that people with a poor diet very clearly have a smaller hippocampus than people with a quality diet. The hippocampus is a part of the brain, shaped like a small seahorse, that is associated with memory and spatial awareness, imagination, creativity, decision-making, empathy, social bonding and language use.

When it comes to the hippocampus, it seems that size *does* matter and is an indication of how well a brain is functioning — so you need to look after yours! As if you needed yet another reason to make sure you have a nourishing diet, particularly when things go pear-shaped. So what should you do right now, while you're waiting for a magic probiotic to fix you up?

Professor Jacka suggests that a diet high in fibre-rich plant-based foods can help restore a bung gut in just *two* weeks. You can also promote a healthy gut by consuming good bacteria in the form of fermented foods such as kimchi, kefir or unpasteurised sauerkraut.

What do you have to lose by giving this a shot?

Foods that boost mood and stave off the blues

Let's get a little more specific. A 2019 study in just over 800 Japanese teenagers found that regularly consuming *green and yellow vegetables* is associated with fewer depressive symptoms. These kids also had a high intake of seaweeds, mushrooms, seafood, light-coloured vegetables in general, potatoes and pickles. Clearly this delicious model bodes well for mental health.

Going for green and yellow

What kinds of green and yellow (and orange) vegetables are we talking? Carrots, pumpkin, corn, sweet potato, green beans, broccoli, zucchini (courgette), kale, rocket (arugula), brussels sprouts, cabbage, watercress, bok choy, silverbeet (Swiss chard), yellow capsicums (peppers), yellow beetroot, squash, yellow potatoes, yellow beans …

Lots of other wholesome foods can also help to keep us on a more even keel by optimising the happiness chemicals in our system — such as serotonin, dopamine and norepinephrine.

Foods that contain antioxidants

Dopamine and serotonin are reduced by oxidation, so antioxidants are a vital part of a good mental health diet, protecting us against oxidative stress and inflammation.

You can get your dose of antioxidants from a range of wholesome foods including berries, tomatoes, citrus fruits, colourful vegetables, onions, potatoes and nuts.

Foods that contain vitamin B

The B group vitamins help our brain produce dopamine and serotonin, and are thought to help protect us against depression. You'll find them in green vegies, eggs, wholegrain bread, milk, lentils, mushrooms, pine nuts, sunflower seeds, salmon, trout, tuna, beef, lamb, chicken, turkey and B12-boosted breakfast cereals. And that's just for starters.

Foods that contain vitamin D

Low levels of vitamin D are linked to depression, and in particular seasonal depression (also known as seasonal affective disorder, or SAD).

Sunlight is the best source of vitamin D, but you can also snaffle some via eggs and dairy foods, as well as drinks and breakfast cereals that have been fortified with vitamin D.

Foods that contain complex carbohydrates

Complex carbohydrates help to stabilise our mood, and they are found in wholegrains, vegetables and fruit. They also promote brain health by regulating the release of glucose into our system.

Foods that contain omega-3 fatty acids

Omega-3s are polyunsaturated fatty acids that help with the production and regulation of the feel-good chemicals dopamine, serotonin and norepinephrine. You'll find omega-3 fatty acids in fish such as salmon, trout, mackerel, anchovies and sardines, eggs, leafy green vegies, walnuts, chia seeds and flaxseed oil.

How am I meant to do all this?

Okay, so now that we know healthy eating sure beats a really crap diet when you're trying to get back on your feet, let's get a bit more real and talk about how and what we might actually end up eating.

Because let's face it, we might not have the resolve, desire or energy to eat wholesomely all the time!

Take it from me, as somebody who loves food ... here are some easy ways to feed yourself when everything else has turned to shite.

How to look after yourself when ordering in

It's important to eat three meals a day when you're on the mend — and it's especially important to have dinner, because otherwise you probably won't sleep well. (I know that having a nutritious dinner really does help me sleep more soundly.)

Sometimes, there's nothing you want more than hot chips or a burger. I get it. I do. So if you find yourself with a box of hot chips sometimes, don't beat yourself up. We're all doing the best we can.

Other times, you may find you have absolutely not one iota of energy and are incapable of cooking yourself a meal. I get that too. It's okay to call in some help, because ordering in is better than not eating at all. And even a semi-nutritious dinner is better than nothing at all.

I know you're too tired to think, so I am thinking for you opposite and over the page, with lots of feel-good ordering-in ideas that are still on the nourishing side.

When you can, try to go for crunchy or lightly cooked options that still have some life and nourishment in them.

Thai

Salads

Stir-fried dishes with simple (rather than sticky/syrupy) sauces

Fresh tofu dishes

Soups

Rice and grilled meats/chicken

Chicken shop

Chicken and salad …

… yes this is totes legit!

Vietnamese

Rice paper rolls

Soups (like pho!)

Rice and grilled meats/chicken

Simple vegie dishes with rice

Japanese

Sushi or sashimi

Salads and fresh tofu dishes

Soups

Edamame

Grilled meats and vegies with rice

Chinese

Soups

Steamed fish

Stir-fried or steamed vegies and rice

Stir-fried dishes in non-sticky or non-syrupy sauces

Steamed dumplings

Mexican

Lean meat or vegetarian burritos, fajitas and tacos

Salads

Guacamole with vegetables

Rice or bean dishes

Italian

Soups and simple salads

Pizza with lots of vegie toppings

Pasta with simple tomato-based sauce

Grilled, lean meats and steamed vegetables

When you can shop and cook, just a little

Okay, there is a bit of cooking here, but it's done in under 5 minutes so it's low effort, which is what we so often want right now.

Supermarket vegie aisle

There are lots of pre-cut vegetable packs here, ready to salad, steam, stir-fry, roast, microwave, turn into a soup … Choose your pre-prepped vegies and do one of the following.

Steam: Do you have a steamer pot? If not, get one; they are brilliant. I got mine at a thrift shop. Or get a bamboo steamer from an Asian grocer.

Stir-fry: A slosh of canola oil in a very hot pan, chuck the vegies in, stir-fry, add garlic, add some sauce (oyster? soy? a stir-fry sauce off the shelf?), stir and stir again, then serve on hot rice. A rice cooker is a good idea, btw. Brown rice will make this even more virtuous, and you can buy it precooked.

Soup: Grab a large diced vegie pack and 1 litre (4 cups) stock. Sizzle a diced onion in oil or butter until soft. Throw in the vegies and fry for a few minutes. Add the stock and cook over medium heat until the vegies are tender. (You can throw in a can of drained beans if you like, too.) Add pepper, scant salt (because stock is already salty) and perhaps some paprika and dried Italian herbs — or fresh if you have them. You can mush it all up with a stick blender if you're going for something extra soothing or have it non-mushed (which I do!).

Roast: Douse chopped vegies in olive oil, toss with garlic cloves and salt and pepper. Add some dried oregano. Pop in the oven and roast on 200°C (400°F), turning now and again, until golden and tender. Splash a wee bit of red wine vinegar over the top. Serve with rocket leaves and a wedge of crusty bread. Maybe a dollop of Greek yoghurt, too?

Microwave: Pop vegies in a bowl with an inch of water in the bottom. Cook on high until tender, depending on the vegie — 3 minutes or so for broccoli and green beans. You can also do frozen vegies like this. Drain and serve hot, tossed in butter and fresh herbs. Or cool and serve with your fave salad dressing. Then, just drizzle with olive oil and a squeeze of lemon and a splash of red wine vinegar. Perhaps some salt and pepper, or sriracha hot sauce or mayo, even?

Salad: Coleslaw packs are a super-easy way to whip up your own non-soggy salad. Just rinse and shake dry. Add your fave salad dressing or make your own. (Some commercial salad dressings are full of crap, so just note that. I am not judging though.)

Freezer aisle

There are lots of **frozen vegie packs** in the freezer aisle, which you can cook according to packet instructions. These are full of nutrients and can sit alongside some barbecued chicken or roast beef from the deli. Perhaps add some spicy sauce or mustard? (If you don't eat meat or chicken, **vegie burgers** and **frozen fish** are also perfectly great. Prepare according to packet and serve with salad.)

Okay, so maybe **Asian dumplings** aren't always super-healthy, but they can make you feel really good when things are rough! I swear they were a brilliant medicine for me when I wasn't feeling my best. I didn't fry them though; I boiled them and had them with chilli and black vinegar and some snipped fresh herbs. YUM. Easy. Quick. Satisfying.

Refrigerated section plus

Fresh pasta is a brilliant choice, especially when paired with a DIY sauce: simmer two 400 g (14 oz) tins of diced tomatoes in juice with a slosh of olive oil, two sliced garlic cloves, a teaspoon of sugar and some herbs (fresh basil or a sprinkling of dried oregano).

Hommus, cheese ... serve with wholegrain crackers or nice grainy bread, a boiled egg, some raw carrot sticks, celery sticks, avocado and cherry tomatoes. So good for you, and you only have to cook the egg!

Falafel ... in a warmed flat bread (buy that too) with hommus, some baby spinach, sliced tomato and cucumber — with some chilli sauce and pickled cabbage (from a jar), perhaps.

Middle grocery aisles throw-together recipes

Tortellini soup
Fry an onion and some sliced garlic in olive oil. Add a small jar of tomato passata, 2 litres (8 cups) stock and half a packet of dried tortellini pasta. Season with salt and pepper and whatever spices and herbs you like — how about sweet paprika and fresh basil? Cook until the pasta is done.

Tuna and rice salad

Mix cold, cooked rice (make it yourself, or buy ready-cooked off the shelf) with a tin of tuna in oil (no need to drain), a tin of corn, some sliced cherry tomatoes, sliced red onion and a handful of frozen peas (nuked for a minute or two). Season with salt, pepper and chilli. Add fresh herbs if you have them.

Simple not-niçoise salad

Microwave or boil a handful of baby potatoes until tender. Microwave or boil green beans until tender. Slice both and let them cool a bit. Pop them in a bowl with a tin of tuna in olive oil (no need to drain) and a sliced red onion. Drizzle with red wine vinegar and a squeeze of kewpie mayo. Garnish with slices of hard-boiled egg if you fancy. Add a small tin of corn if you like, or some cherry tomatoes. Just do your thing.

Roasted cherry tomatoes with pesto and pasta

In a hot oven, roast some cherry tomatoes (a punnet or two) with a good drizzle of olive oil and whatever dried herbs you have. Cook some pasta. Tip the roasted tomatoes/oil onto the pasta with a spoonful of ready-made pesto. Season with salt and pepper, and grated cheese if you fancy. Eat with crusty bread.

Note that Professor Felice Jacka has heaps more ideas on how to feed yourself for optimal brain health in that book I mentioned before, *Brain Changer*.

When you can't cook at all

- Crispbread topped with sliced tomato, hommus, cheese, salt and pepper.

- Open a tin of tuna in olive oil. Mix with half a punnet of halved cherry tomatoes and a small chopped cucumber. Add mayo and hot sauce if you fancy, plus salt and pepper.

- Grainy bread topped with avocado and lemon juice, and a sprinkling of salt and pepper.

- A pre-cooked tub of brown rice with half a tin of corn kernels, a small chopped cucumber, a few sliced cherry tomatoes, and some mayo or Greek yoghurt.

- Cheese on toast! Try to use wholegrain bread and maybe slide some tomato slices underneath for a little vegie boost.

CHAPTER 9

How nature and movement might help

Feeling slumpy and indoorsy?

EVERYTHING IN THIS chapter is detailed as something that *may* help lift your spirits. You may not feel like doing any of them right now, so please just come back to them whenever you're ready.

It really sucks when you are suffering and someone tells you to go for a walk to clear your head.

As sensible as that advice can be, it's not always practical, or useful, and is often downright irritating, right?

Well actually, there's a plethora of studies that prove that spending time in the natural world really can help us feel better.

Spending time outside helps to recapture our attention, which is especially helpful when things are hard. Trees, the ocean, the mountains somehow begin to mend us. They're a helpful 'tonic of big things'. (More on that coming up!)

Humans have never really needed studies to confirm this, though. Each of us knows that time spent outside is very often a helpful, grounding and distracting salve.

There are a few theories as to why we find nature so bolstering, and indeed why it can soothe us when we're feeling shite.

Let's explore some of these together …

We humans have
an inbuilt urge to
seek connections
with nature.

'We are secret Neanderthals'

One theory as to why nature soothes us is that we have evolved to maintain a strong connection with the natural world because our survival once depended on knowing what might lay between those trees or under that rock. Being immersed in environments we've evolved to be part of can make us feel more at home. I call it the 'We are secret Neanderthals' theory.

A more distinguished version of this, the 'biophilia' hypothesis, suggests we humans have an inbuilt urge to seek connections with nature, and to 'affiliate with other forms of life'. Literally, 'biophilia' means 'love of life', or 'love of living systems'.

This term was popularised by the brilliant American biologist and conservationist Edward Osborne Wilson, in his 1984 book *Biophilia*. As he famously wrote, 'Nature holds the key to our aesthetic, intellectual, cognitive and even spiritual satisfaction.'

E.O. Wilson has gone on to win loads of awards for his work, including a couple of Pulitzer Prizes, so he knows what he's talking about.

Shinrin-yoku:
Japanese forest bathing

The Japanese have also long understood our innate connection with the natural world. In recent decades, this has given rise to a practice called shinrin-yoku, or 'forest bathing'. Perhaps you have heard of it? It describes a form of healing therapy that involves being in a forest and soaking up the forest atmosphere with all one's senses.

Shinrin-yoku is not about racking up steps on an activity tracker, but rather simply reconnecting to nature and grounding ourselves in something much bigger than us. Immersing ourselves in a forest's smells, sounds, colours, light, patterns, texture, temperature and character helps us to connect to the earth and to ourselves.

'Let nature enter through your ears, eyes, nose, mouth, hands and feet,' writes Dr Qing Li in *TIME* magazine. 'Drink in the flavour of the forest and release your sense of joy and calm. This is your sixth sense, a state of mind. Now you have connected with nature. You have crossed the bridge to happiness.' Dr Qing Li is president of the Japanese Society for Forest Medicine and author of *Forest Bathing: How Trees Can Help You Find Health and Happiness*.

And if you don't live near a forest, don't fret, he says. Once you've grasped the gentle, meditative fundamentals — soaking up the elements of nature, looking at plants, dipping your toes in a stream, watching birds — you can 'forest bathe' anywhere there are trees, such as a nearby park or garden, and in any kind of weather. Scientific studies have shown that forest bathing can reduce blood pressure, stress (as measured by cortisol levels), depression, fatigue and anxiety, and improve mood, concentration, energy and quality of sleep, and even boost our immunity.

These are all issues you might be grappling with just now — so perhaps a self-prescribed dose of nature might be just what Dr You ordered?

South Korea's healing forests

Getting back to trees again … in her book *The Nature Fix*, journalist Florence Williams writes about how, in a similar vein to Japanese forest bathing, South Korea has been planting dozens of 'healing forests' for its citizens, and is developing a billion-dollar forest healing complex.

And South Korea's healing forests are proving similarly beneficial.

Florence describes two South Korean studies in young teens who were borderline technology addicts. After trips to the forest of two days each, the teens had lower levels of the stress hormone cortisol, as well as greatly improved self-esteem — and these benefits lasted for two weeks. The kids also reported feeling happier and less anxious.

Yet another reason to spend some time in nature, when you can.

Nature as a salve

There are lots of theories as to why connecting with nature benefits us in so many ways, and personally I believe them all. I've spent a lot of time sitting by bushy tracks because of elements of each of them.

The 'attention restoration theory' (ART) by Rachel and Stephen Kaplan suggests that exposure to nature — and even *pictures* of nature — helps replenish our frazzled brains. By fully capturing our attention, nature shuts the overwhelm and stressful distractions of daily life out and leaves us feeling restored.

And in fact, studies show people who are able to catch a glimpse of the natural world heal more quickly, feel less pain and are more positive and calmer, too.

Roger Ulrich's 'stress reduction theory' suggests that the sky, earth, water, trees and other natural elements are innately calming, and that's why we feel more like ourselves after we've spent time amongst them.

As with forest bathing, these scenarios that involve immersion in nature hinge on the idea that these environments help to moderate an upsetting state of arousal and dull or divert negative thoughts. This in turn reduces physical and mental stress symptoms.

Scientists are finding physical proof of this phenomenon, too. A 2015 study at Stanford University found that a 90-minute walk in a natural setting reduced activity in the part of the brain that ruminates on things — the subgenual prefrontal cortex — whereas a 90-minute walk in an urban area did not have the same effect.

Another factor in this 'nature as salve' phenomenon is that many people have a spiritual connection to nature — or a specific place — due to their history or heritage.

This connection to place or country can help promote spiritual health and prove restorative, both physically and mentally.

And look, to me it makes a lot of sense that taking life back to basics — spending time in the natural world away from stressful situations — is going to provide some perspective and good feels. It might also perhaps spark some important thoughts about simplifying life and connecting to what is truly meaningful and important to us.

Or it may spark crying. That's okay too. While you're sobbing, you might be healing a little bit, so all is not lost and hooray for helpful trees.

Prescribing a dose of nature

The Scottish government is even encouraging doctors to dispense 'nature prescriptions' for their patients to reduce health problems such as high blood pressure and anxiety.

On their Healthy Shetland website, as part of RSPB Scotland's Nature Prescriptions, is a brilliant monthly calendar list of outdoorsy suggestions people can undertake, and it's helpful and incredibly specific, including:

- Stand looking over the Loch of Belmont in Unst and listen to the pre-migratory courtship of calloos (long-tailed ducks) before they move north to their tundra breeding grounds.

- Don't mow the lawn — and watch the mini-beasts move in.

- Create a rock sculpture on a beach.

- Follow a bumblebee.

- Re-wild one of your senses — smell everything in nature.

- Write a worry onto a stone and throw it into the sea.

- Get out 'whatever the weather' and feel the exhilaration of wind and rain on your face.

- Make a bird bath — an upside-down bin lid will do.

(I'm super-keen for us to create a list like this for all kinds of places; perhaps you could head to my website and share your ideas under the 'My Nature Prescription' button?)

Create your own prescription for nice times

Shake off the self-judgement and take some time to think about what makes you feel terrible, what makes you feel great, and what your energy levels look like at different times of the day. Make notes for a day or two, to build a good picture of how you do *you*.

What can you tweak for optimal ace-ness?

Do you need to sleep more, or eat more regularly?

Are you pushing yourself too hard?

Do you need to work on that nagging voice inside your head?

Do you need to rethink how you are responding to a toxic person?

Do you need to make more tea cosies? Or listen to more music?

See more of your pals? Or less?

Or make more pots of delicious tea?

Is mindfulness something you might like to explore?

Then, write yourself a prescription for happiness. In fact, why not write several prescriptions, for right now, and further down the track, to ensure you fit in some everyday activities and habits that boost your happiness quota?

Think about …

- a **daily** prescription for small things to do to increase your creativity and wellbeing

- a **weekly** prescription for those things you should try to slip in once a week to boost your wellbeing

- a **monthly** prescription for things that are less important, but still good to have in your life

- an **annual** prescription for *much* wanted or hoped-for events or things.

Try not to get too ambitious, because you've gotta be practical, and you probably have limited energy right now. So start small and make it manageable. For instance, your prescriptions could be 'weekly library visit' or 'daily yoga' or 'a poem a day' or 'monthly visit to gallery' or 'daily drawing' or 'weekly lunch with fave person' or 'monthly psych visit' or 'annual solo retreat'. Just keep them unique and meaningful to you.

Build in some movement

It can be hard to get moving when you're feeling like a piece of poop. But please make an effort to squeeze in a bit of love for your physical being, in a way that works for you, because it will make you feel better in the long run. Perhaps it's doing 5 minutes of yoga each day (a little goes a long way!), to remind your body that there are muscles and blood and organs that wouldn't mind a little bit of attention? Perhaps it's a gentle walk around the block or your local park? You don't have to turn into a gym junkie — just give yourself permission to tackle movement in your own way.

Food is your friend

You can waste an awful lot of time obsessing about the morality
of food and beating yourself up over 'good' and 'bad' snacks.
Please don't. Instead try, with all your might, to both nourish and
forgive yourself when it comes to eating. Love yourself by cooking
yummy food from scratch and eating it happily. Or by buying your
favourite treats from the shops and eating them happily.

Remember to breathe

If you are feeling stressed-out or anxious, you are probably not
breathing very deeply, and perhaps even holding your breath
without meaning to? When we breathe in a shallow way, it actually
keeps our body in a state of stress and creates tension in our
shoulders and neck. Deep breathing, using your diaphragm,
lowers your blood pressure, relaxes your muscles, increases your
energy levels and is wonderfully grounding — so make an effort
to notice your breathing whenever you are feeling tizzy or anxious.
Slow down and take a few deep breaths.

You could download an app that helps you focus on breathing
deeply, or try some yoga breathing? Or try walking more
and breathing more rhythmically? There are even breathing
therapies you can sign up for. Or you could just, you know, lie on
your bed and concentrate on breathing for a few minutes each day
without any of these fancy bells and whistles.

It feels really good to breathe properly because it allows your
body to work the way it should, and is deeply calming for both
mind and body.

A tonic of big things

My great-grandfather Frank W. Boreham did his own fair share of communing in nature, especially in Tasmania, Victoria and New Zealand.

'We have the trees as teachers and preachers, and many a man has learned the deepest lessons of his life at the feet of these shrewd and silent philosophers,' Frank said of trees (and I'm sure he meant of women, too).

He advocated for spending time in nature taking in the 'tonic of big things' and creating a little distance between ourselves and our troubles.

'Immensity is magnificent medicine; that is one reason ... why the doctors send us to the seaside,' Frank wrote. 'We forget the tiddley-winking in the contemplation of the tremendous; we lose life's shallow worries in the vision of unplumbed depths.'

And he saw the migration of birds as further proof that the natural world affects us in ways we might not be completely conscious of.

'We are all affected more than we know by forces that we cannot see,' Frank said. 'Crocuses break through the snow; nodding daffodils smother the bank; yellow primroses carpet the leafy woods; bluebells swarm along the hedgerows; and the birds sing their mating-songs in utter indifference to the horror of the world's stark tragedy,' he wrote.

I must admit some parts of Frank's writings are a little too devout for me, but when I was feeling my worst I would sift through his books and editorials looking for words of wisdom from someone connected — by blood — to me.

Even though I never met him, it felt like his writing had been waiting for me ... and so many of his observations about human nature and life acted as a sort of familial salve.

'We get over things,' my great-grandpa Frank promised in his book *Mushrooms on the Moor*. 'It is the most amazing faculty that we possess. War or pestilence; drought or famine; fire or flood; it does not matter. However devastating the catastrophe, however frightful the slaughter, however total the eclipse, we surmount our sorrows and find ourselves still smiling when the storm is overpast.'

As Frank concludes, 'Nature heals her wounds with loveliness.'

And maybe with her loveliness, Nature can heal our wounds, too.

Thank you, Frank!

Eco-therapy

The term 'eco-therapy' (also known as 'nature therapy' or 'green therapy') describes nature-based programs that promote physical and mental good health while doing outdoorsy kinds of things. Think lots of fresh air, rustling branches, rushing rivers, squawking birds and avoiding animal droppings, and you're on the right track.

Independent activity or more formalised programs include stuff like gardening, caring for animals, adventure and wilderness activities, hiking, walking and crafting — in or with nature.

Immersing yourself in these sorts of eco-therapy activities has been found to help relax the nervous system, reduce depression, anger and anxiety, and improve mood, self-esteem and resilience.

Depending on the sort of eco-therapy you opt for, you might find yourself being able to process your feelings with more clarity away from the usual distractions. It may help to shift your perspective, forge new routines and just feel more grounded and relaxed. If you choose a social activity, you have the benefit of making new connections and feeling part of something bigger.

Remember that nature has a way of putting things back into perspective.

As psychologist Oliver James noted, in a brilliant piece on eco-therapy for *The Guardian* in 2014: 'The egocentricity of clients is often reduced by awareness of something much bigger than them, whether it be mountains, wide open plains or huge skies. The feeling that the client is the centre of the universe is called into question by the sheer scale and complexity of nature.'

Yet another way of saying that nature has a way of putting things back into perspective.

Ponder going a little further afield. Cold days are brilliant for more contemplative walks when there are fewer humans around. (If you're going somewhere pretty remote, though, always tell someone trusty where you're going. We don't want to see you on the news being winched to safety!)

My own eco-therapy took a literary direction. Even though I didn't feel I had the energy or fortitude to venture too far into the wilderness, I couldn't stop reading about it and reminding myself that there were bigger things than me. So I stayed home a lot and read books about other people who went outside a lot. I really loved *The Sheep Stell* by Janet White, about her solitary life raising sheep on a tiny island in New Zealand, and *H is for Hawk* by Helen Macdonald, detailing her efforts to train a stroppy goshawk in the midst of insular grief.

Maybe books about nature will help soothe your frazzled soul, too.

HOME-BASED ECO-THERAPY

Perhaps you are too tired, sad or anxious to venture far from home? You can still tap into the benefits of nature-focused pursuits close to home.

- Buy some binoculars — and no, don't spy on your neighbours, but on the bird life around your home.

- Commune with the bees by cultivating plants they like or leaving bee snacks out for them.

- Put some herb pots on a window ledge and grow your own mini kitchen garden. There's something encouraging about watching things grow and plucking fresh some leaves to put in your spaghetti. Or sprout some seeds on the window ledge.

- Find some time each day to get out into the street or garden and feel the light and fresh air on your face.

- Buy or rescue some neglected plants and take them home into natural light.

- Download some relaxing rain playlists and listen to them when you're in the bath or snuggled down in bed or on a couch.

- Grow some vegetables if you have space outside, or indoors in pots; if you're not sure what varieties are suitable, chat to your local nursery staff or a green-thumbed friend.

- Tune into a wildlife cam. I love Decorah Eagles, which has been going for many years and is watched by thousands across the globe.

- Cultivate a sourdough starter and bake your own bread.

- Put a bird bath or nesting box in your garden.

- When you're out walking, sneakily snip a few leaves and flowers to pop into a vase at home.

- Plant some sunflower seeds.

Water therapy

Perhaps you remember those photos of Prince Harry, Duke of Sussex, hanging out with his new wife Duchess Meghan on Sydney's Bondi Beach?

That was more than a colourful photo opportunity. Prince Harry has long been a mental health advocate, and the royals were attending a Fluro Friday run by OneWave, a non-profit surf community support group that aims to destigmatise mental health challenges and get people out in the water so they can discover the soul-healing benefits of surf therapy.

Surfing the waves

Champion surfer Layne Beachley is another passionate advocate for the gains that taking to the ocean can bring. After being diagnosed with chronic fatigue syndrome and then clinical depression, it was surfing that helped her recover.

'Diving in the ocean, I feel this sense of being cleansed from my head all the way down to my toes ... almost like it cleanses my mind, my body and my soul,' she told the ABC radio program, *All In The Mind*.

'It's a place where I feel connected. It's a place where I feel a sense of freedom. And as a self-confessed control freak, it's a great place to surrender, because it's a force way more powerful than me.'

The US Navy is also researching the benefits of surf therapy for treating personnel with sleep disorders, post-traumatic stress disorder and depression.

Wallow in the tub

Perhaps you're not the surfing type? That's okay. There's so much more to water as a healing buddy that doesn't involve an impossibly snug wetsuit.

If you can't make it to the beach or river or lake, you can simply hop in the shower to feel some of the benefits water can bring. The sound and feel of the shower can help spark the same sort of feel-good, grounding reaction that being in actual nature does.

We've already talked a little about the therapeutic benefits of hot baths, including hot springs. I used to think it was the feeling of being warm and enveloped that made me feel better after a bath when I was feeling my worst.

Turns out it's far more than that. As we've seen, hot baths — as well as long, hot showers — cause blood to rush to our skin surface, away from our core, and it is this drop in core body temperature that helps relax us really efficiently, and later nod off to sleep. Hot baths and showers are also thought to promote healthy circadian rhythms — *possibly* by providing a warm boost that tells our body that it's daytime. (And consequently providing a kind of 'reset', which may signal night time, and sleep, more clearly to our muddled-up bodies and brains.)

Some research (admittedly on rats, but let's go with it) also suggests that increases in body temperature fire up serotonin-releasing neurons in the part of the brain that regulates mood. Serotonin is a feel-good hormone, and people who have low levels often suffer from depression. So as well as normalising your circadian rhythm, that cosy bath or long, hot shower might be boosting your serotonin levels, too.

And it seems that floating about in water also has some other brain benefits, by encouraging calming theta brainwaves to kick in. These brainwaves are slow frequency and push us into a state we more readily zone out and daydream in.

These theta brain waves also happen when we are in a deep meditative state or in the light stage of sleep. They also kick in when we're doing tasks that are so automatic that we are able to mentally disengage from them, such as when running, or driving familiar stretches along the freeway. This theta state is about free flow ... a sort of meditation in the everyday.

Apparently these theta waves can also be sparked in the shower, bath or even while shaving your legs or face!

The calm blue mind

Marine biologist Wallace J. Nichols also talks about the remarkable benefits of being in, under or simply near water, and its ability to diminish anxiety.

In his book *Blue Mind*, Wallace explains that both our visual and auditory stimulation are simplified when we're around water, giving our brains a chance to relax and defrag — and letting us connect with our innate 'blue mind', which he describes as 'a mildly meditative state characterised by calm, peacefulness, unity, and a sense of general happiness and satisfaction with life in the moment'.

This 'blue mind' state is switched on when we're in or around water, particularly in nature, and this connection with nature can help activate our daydreamy, imaginative, soft-focus state.

Like many others, Wallace believes that the sense of awe and wonder we experience when surrounded by nature — water, in this case — sparks an important and fortifying perspective shift, and gives us that 'one with the universe' feeling.

It's a surefire way of giving your churning brain a break from playing current misfortunes over and over in your mind.

The theta state
is about
free flow ...
a sort of
meditation
in the everyday.

Dive like a mammal

Water is so brilliant in the feel-better stakes that even just splashing some on your bare face can help.

Yup. Humans share something with otters and seals (and other diving animals) called the mammalian diving reflex. It helps humans to dive underwater more effectively and sparks when our faces are submerged in cold water.

It also kicks in when you simply splash cold water on your face, prompting your heart rate to slow, and sending blood to your vital organs, and helping to stave off anxiety.

If a splash of cold water on your face sounds way too bracing, just wipe your face with a warm, gentle cloth and let's call that a bloody good effort. You've got a lot on your plate now, so you can slowly work up to being a seal or an otter ...

The right light

I'm sure you already know that getting into natural light and the cosy glow of sunny sunshine is proven to make us feel better.

Our exposure to cycles of light and darkness is important for synchronising our circadian rhythm — our natural 24-hour biological clock that governs our many intricate physiological cycles and processes, including our core body temperature, sleep cycles, how our cells function and hormone secretion.

One such hormone is melatonin, which is usually produced when night falls, or a little later if you are a teenager — and later still if you are a wakeful adult with an iPad or laptop propped in front of your face until all hours.

There is growing evidence that when our circadian rhythm is out of whack, our mood, metabolism and other functions are affected.

In ye olden days, before we were surrounded with artificial lighting, it was easy for our circadian rhythm to sync naturally with the sun. But now we're surrounded by all kinds of light emitting from streets, surrounding buildings, our hallway night-light, our phones, our laptops, the neighbour's floodlights and more.

You might think that the light from your laptop when you're hunkered down for the fifth night in a row watching your favourite online show is making you *feel* a little more at peace in the world for a while — but it might also be contributing to your wakeful nights and sadness in the long term. Sorrrryyyy!

The intensity of light is measured in lux units. A laptop emits over 33,000 per cent more lux units than a full moon! Geesh.

Researchers think there may well be a correlation between the increase in night-time lighting and an increase in mood disorders and sleep problems.

So when you're nursing yourself through a hard time, remember that light at night has a detrimental effect on humans, so it's a good idea to try to optimise your sleep environment so that light isn't messing with your already beleaguered body.

Perhaps you might want to read a book at bedtime instead? Or turn out all the lights and listen to the radio … or the rain on the roof … or just the night-time sounds if they don't creep you out. (They creep me out.)

All this light is messing up not only the body rhythms of humans, but the habitat, behaviour and life cycles of many animals. Plants are affected too. Sigh. So if you won't reduce the lights at your place for *you*, maybe you could do it for the wellness of the plants and animals (big and small) that live in your vicinity.

Pet therapy

While we're talking about animals, let's talk about something less sad than light pollution. Let's talk about the restorative medicine that is ... pet therapy!

If you can't have your own pet, you could always find other ways to bond with or observe animals, and have their non-judgmental presence in your orbit.

A review of a bunch of studies on the benefits of pets for people experiencing mental health challenges noted that animals encouraged their owners to stay in the present — avoiding worry and ruminations about past behaviours or concerns about the future. Pets were also found to increase physical activity and promote time spent outdoors and with nature. And as we know — because we've read this far in the book and are geniuses — these are very good habits for people who are feeling not so good.

Having a pet also meant their owners had more social interaction with others, fostering a sense of connectedness within their community.

The loyal, consistent and proximate presence of a pet provides companionship and support. This feeling of closeness and connection between pet and human was intensified by the common belief that animals instinctively know when their owners need them and act accordingly. Pet owners found this incredibly soothing during difficult times.

I personally have found sharing affection with a pet to be incredibly helpful during my hard times. There are only so many hugs you can give your kids and buddies before they get a little irritated and remind you of their personal space.

Patting a pet can help lower your heart rate, which is especially good if you suffer from anxiety.

Pets also provide a routine framework because they need to be cared for each day ... this is a great baseline for your day if you are sometimes prone to forget about looking after yourself. Pets lead you by example.

My dog, Bean, is honestly up for as many hugs and kisses as I can muster and looks at me with more love than anyone in the world. There's something very fortifying about being adored, and it also seems to kick in those feel-good hormones (in both of us) that help to snap me out of trickier thought processes, and remind me that parts of the world are indeed wholesome and good. If a little licky.

The experts confirm that the benefits I speak of are indeed a total THING. #ScienceWantsYouToGetAPet

Therapy animals are being used in a wide variety of settings — from schools, hospitals and nursing homes to mental health units — to help offer emotional support and relief to people dealing with all kinds of circumstances.

It's not just dogs either, but chickens, ponies, rabbits, pigs, cats, reptiles ... So great are the ensuing bonds that people have been known to travel with a turkey and even a peacock as their emotional support animal, so apparently the sky is not the limit.

In short, there are a lot of fuzzy and fluffy snuggles going on.

And if your circumstances right now don't allow you to have your own support animal, you could always consider volunteering at an animal shelter or similar to bring some Good Boy and Good Girl pets into your life.

Or why not watch some cute videos featuring soul-cheering animals, or simply say hello to the pets you see in your travels?

'Hello, puppy!'

'Good day, peacock!'

CHAPTER 10

Do you need some professional support?

Sometimes you need more than self-care.

Sometimes you need to call in the professionals.

FOR A WHILE there, I was still able to focus on the good bits of life, however sporadically. I took pretty pictures of things that made me feel nice. I made things because making things made me feel nice, but even these trusty strategies were not enough one day.

I felt myself tumbling into a place where very little was nice, and the idea of doing normal things seemed truly impossible. I was crippled with anxiety and a bewildered foggy numbness, and crying, a *lot*. I just sort of wanted to hide away and be left alone, to feel better. And alarmingly, all the things I liked to do, feel, eat … I just didn't want to do anymore.

That was the catalyst for me — the point at which I realised I couldn't heal *me*, and I needed to get some help.

But honestly, you don't need to get to a crisis point to benefit from some extra support from a therapist. In fact, it's good to reach out before you feel like a bag of freaked-out poop.

Health psychologist Dr Jo Abbott says only about one in three Australians with mental health difficulties obtain help — and I'm guessing this is pretty similar in other Western countries, too. She suggests there are lots of practical reasons for this low uptake, such as access to health professionals, time and travel issues, financial restrictions — and also because there's still a bit of a stigma attached to accessing mental support.

Please don't feel ashamed or embarrassed to reach out. It's not an admission of 'failure' — and you really don't have to go through it all alone.

When to see a GP or a therapist

When we're going through a really challenging time, it's normal to experience a whole gamut of negative feelings that we usually try to avoid — such as feeling anxious, scared, angry, panicked, overwhelmed, confused, disoriented, apathetic, disconnected, exhausted, pessimistic, depressed, hypervigilant, hypersensitive, worthless, erratic, having intrusive negative thoughts, having difficulty concentrating or remembering things ...

Yikes, that's a lot!

Just remember that as awful as all this sounds and feels — in each of these is a message. It's your body letting you know that things are amiss and you need to take care.

But if you — like me — need some kind of checklist to measure your own symptoms against when deciding whether to seek professional support, here are some red flags, as suggested by the Victorian government on their 'Better Health' website.

Don't listen to me, listen to the experts. As they say, if these symptoms persist, you really must get some extra help and find someone to help you work through this hard time.

PLEASE SEEK SUPPORT IF YOU ARE EXPERIENCING ANY OF THE FOLLOWING FOR LONGER THAN A FEW WEEKS:

- Feeling unable to deal with intense feelings or physical sensations.

- Feeling consistently anxious, on edge or easily startled.

- You aren't having normal feelings, but are instead feeling numb and empty.

- You keep suffering from physical stress symptoms.

- You are having continued disturbed sleep or even nightmares.

- You are avoiding situations that might trigger memories or hard feelings.

- You feel unsupported, or unable to share your feelings with others.

- You are having trouble relating to friends or family.

- You are more accident-prone than usual.

- You are using alcohol or drugs more than usual.

- Feeling unable to work, or deal with everyday responsibilities.

- You continue to go over hard things you have experienced.

How does it feel when you first reach out for help?

Look it's hard. I felt sick for a week. I cried. But I knew it was important for me to seek out some professional help. How did I know?

Well ... I couldn't stop crying, to be honest.

One day I was driving my son Ari to work. We were speeding along the freeway listening to music and Ari said something totally not upsetting; tears just started streaming down my face and I began sobbing. I didn't want him to see, so I was trying to drive with my head turned away, while still keeping my eyes on the road.

So I took myself off to the doctor.

If you've ever done what I did, you will know that ...

a)
it hurts your neck

b)
it's not very safe, and

c)
it's bewildering for anyone else in the car — and anyone zipping by who happens upon your cryface!

What happens next, after you shuffle into the doctor's room and begin talking about what's been going on?

Well, there are a couple of quizzes to gauge how you are feeling, and the ways in which you might need help. I did one at the GP's when the doctor signed off on my mental health plan, and another one at the psychologist's to determine how anxious and depressed I might be.

It's a bit challenging to see questions capturing your thoughts and feelings in black and white like that, but I just whizzed through them as quickly and honestly as I could so that ...

a)
I didn't overthink it

b)
I captured what I was actually going through, without trying to make it seem less crap.

I wrote about this experience straight afterwards, and I'll share it with you on the next few pages, to give you an idea of how it felt.

Today I went to the doctor to spill the deep dark secret that I cannot fix myself all by myself. It was hard, I'm not gonna lie.

Firstly, I want to believe that you can fix yourself if you pay attention and do all the things that nourish you but ...

Secondly, that is not always true. Sigh.

It's definitely correct that I waited way too long to go to the doctor. But I am an optimist and it takes me a while to realise that not everything will sort itself out.

My doctor was really very nice considering I had not seen her in approximately eight years. I know. Yep. What?

It's just that I had been so busy holding things together that the idea of telling someone who *knows about stuff* that I was not okay felt like it would break me into tiny pieces.

I know the idea is to put things back together, going to the doctor and all, but for me it felt like if I admitted how awful I was feeling, everything would crumble and a whole alternate universe would open up and not the *good* kind of alternate universe.

But the thing was that I was not feeling better, and furthermore I was feeling less hopeful.

So I booked another appointment with my doctor — a long one — and for the 10 days preceding it I practised different ways to talk about all the things that seemed wrong with me. I lay awake at night worrying about how to say the correct things that would get me the correct care in the allotted 30 minutes. It was a good distraction from my actual worries, to be honest, and in the end I wrote a list of my problems — physical and otherwise — so I wouldn't go off track if I could not stop crying.

In the end, I *did* go off track and I *did* cry, but I was able to rein myself in enough to rattle out some idea of what I had been going through. From the kind responses of my doctor, it was clear to me that I was being pretty hard on myself, and heavy on the disappointment in myself.

Just like in the movies, she handed me a tissue. It was actually the last tissue in the box, which I found helpful because we had time constraints and I knew I had to pace myself because there was only one tissue.

The list I'd written beforehand helped because when I was trying to stop crying, the doctor could glance at it and guide me to the next thing. Thank goodness for lists.

What I left with was:

    a.   the name of a psychologist written on a piece of paper

    b.   a bandaid on my arm, mopping up a tiny dot of red from a blood test

    c.   another appointment 10 days later

    d.   a sheet explaining what antidepressants are, and

    e.   a giant flood of tears being held back by a tiny speck of willpower.

I had a much-too-little cry in the car on the way home, and then I felt a weird empty-nothing-numb calm wash over me — one that I now know is dissociation.

I rang the psychologist and cheerily booked my appointment. She got me in the very next day.

How does it feel to see a psychologist for the first time?

When I went for the first time, I wrote about that, too. Here is what I wrote.

Today I went to the psychologist to spill the deep dark secret that I cannot fix myself all by myself. It was pretty hard, I'm not gonna lie.

I was early of course, because part of my coping mechanism is to be early enough to allow for any contingencies.

I was so early that I switched parking spots twice and went to a bookshop before I set off across the bonkers five-pointed Kew Junction crossing.

And then I was early into the building foyer, where there helpfully was a small café, but I didn't want to stop lest I was late to the top floor of the building and to my appointment.

I was early into the consultation rooms, too. There was just a couch and the hum of voices and a loud radio and two closed doors.

I sat there for a minute and realised that I needed to look at my phone because the panicked feeling was threatening to fizz through my whole body and whoosh out of my chest, no matter how hard I clenched my teeth.

After 10 minutes of looking at my phone and chanting the words on the screen in my head to avoid any *thoughts* coming in to whip up the panic, one of the doors opened and a lady slipped out of the room and out the door.

I just looked at her knees.

Then the psychologist ducked out of view for a minute, leaving the door open. And then she ducked back into view and greeted me warmly, inviting me to come in.

And in I went, into a room with a few nice chairs and a lovely view and a kind face that was ready to listen and ask questions.

Honestly? I had been mulling over how it would go. What I would need to say. What was the right way to do it. Should I make another list?

But in the end it was more about settling in and surrendering in a sort of active way … and getting some help with filing thoughts and feelings into piles to look at today — or another day.

Finally getting to fight through the fog and panic and sadness, and examine what lies beneath was part confronting and part relief.

For me it was mostly relief, to be honest. Because coping mechanisms had been holding life in place with sticky tape and blu tack and a bit of hot glue gun action.

Unpicking all that and examining what there was to work with — and how ingenious our coping skills can be, and how resilience can help us hang on — felt sad, but ultimately hopeful and cleansing.

I thought an hour would zip by, but it plodded slowly as we plotted where I had been, where I was and where I might like to go (the latter was still pretty unclear, I admit!).

I left feeling a sort of suspicious gladness — like I was squinting to see a potentially better view, knowing that there would be a lot of ground to cover … but that there was a person that would hike along with me and help me over the bumpy bits.

What if you're really worried about getting professional help?

During a couple of sessions where we talked about what was going on in my brain, I also chatted to my psychologist, Christina, about the fact that lots of people might have misgivings about seeing a therapist.

(I waited a while to ask her this, because I didn't want her to think my sessions were a ruse to get an expert opinion for this book! They honestly were not, and thankfully Christina knows this.)

But back to the reluctant-yet-suffering souls. Why don't they feel therapy would help them?

Perhaps they've watched a lot of movies where therapy seems uncomfortable or confrontational.

Perhaps they fear that therapy will set them a series of challenges that they must get right.

Perhaps — like me — they fear that once they begin to unravel the things that are weighing on them, they will fall apart.

I honestly had almost every misunderstanding possible about what therapy would be like. I think I was projecting what I was feeling about myself onto everyone else, including my future psychologist.

In reality I should have been getting help *ten years earlier*. That's a long time to suffer because of misconceptions and fear.

During our sessions I asked Christina what she'd say to people who are considering seeing a psychologist.

A FEW THINGS I PULLED OUT OF
OUR CONVERSATION WERE:

- It's important to find someone you are comfortable with, because it's an important relationship. You don't have to go into a lot of detail in your first session, but rather get to know each other and see if it feels right. Then you can dive a little deeper.

- Sessions are not designed to expose you or make you feel even more vulnerable and broken — regardless of what you see on TV.

- Your relationship with your psychologist is a partnership that prioritises your mental health. It's putting two heads together to help one. (And you are the one!)

- Your psychologist will never ever judge you. Instead they will provide a supportive environment for you to excavate how you are feeling.

- Your psychologist is also there to help you find new ways of looking at familiar things when you are struggling.

I would like to add that if your thoughts are in a bit of a loop all the time, this calm and logical reframing from a compassionate professional really can help to shift that.

Christina helped me to organise my thoughts, and made constructive but kind observations when she noticed me getting a bit stuck in a pattern of thinking badly about myself. She also helped me look at some new strategies for looking after my mental health, told me about some concepts surrounding compassion that were really helpful, and made me realise how important it was for me to understand that I was not alone in the awful aftermath of my tough time.

When I started writing this book, I chatted by email with another psychologist, Kerry Athanasiadis, who happened to be a member of a craft group I started years ago called Brown Owls. She was a student psychologist when she'd joined, but was now fully qualified, and so I tapped her on the shoulder because I love it that things can come full circle *and* I wanted to ask her for some advice for the therapy-phobic.

'What would you tell a person who was a bit scared about the idea of reaching out for help from a psychologist?' I wanted to know.

Here is what Kerry wrote back.

1. It's totally normal and natural to feel nervous when you meet a complete stranger to talk about personal or sensitive stuff that you've been struggling with. It takes a lot of courage and strength to take that first step and reach out for support, so give yourself some credit for that!

    The first session is nothing scary. Your psychologist usually just wants to get to know you and understand your presenting issues. They will ask you some basic questions like: Who is in your family? Who do you live with? Do you study/ work? What are your hobbies and interests? And so on. Usually towards the end of the session you will set some goals together, for what you'd like to get out of the sessions. In the first session, you don't have to go into any detail about anything you don't feel comfortable talking about. Usually you will just stick to the headlines, not the details (especially if your support issues are related to trauma).

    If you're really, really nervous, sometimes your psychologist will be able to offer you some alternative options to start off with, like communicating over the phone or through email to begin with, until you feel comfortable coming in to meet in person. They will also usually have a quick chat on the phone with you to introduce themselves and explain their counselling approach.

2. The counselling room is a safe, non-judgmental space and your psychologist is trained to provide you with unconditional positive regard. We have heard lots of different stories and support issues that people might otherwise feel embarrassed to share outside of the counselling room. We know that all human beings have vulnerabilities and that sharing your story with someone in a safe space dissipates that shame and fosters connection. We are here to help, so we want you to know that it is a great privilege to hold space for you and to hear your story.

3. We will never do anything in counselling that you're not 100% comfortable with. Every therapeutic intervention, technique, strategy or exercise will be explained to you clearly so you can give informed consent. Everyone is different, so it is not a one-size-fits all approach. Most psychologists will tailor a therapy plan to suit your needs. For example, some people might want practical tools and skills to create change, whereas other people might want to talk and get things off their chest in a safe space with someone they trust, which can be therapeutic in itself. Some people might want a lot of homework and things to try outside of the counselling room, while others may prefer to take it slow and try activities and exercises together with their psychologist. It really all depends on what you would find helpful or what you have found to be helpful in the past.

4. Finally, I guess I would want people to know that whatever they are experiencing doesn't have to be a life-sentence. Anxiety and depression are very common, and most people do completely recover from both! There are so many different things we can do to help in counselling to get you to a place where you're feeling better and more hopeful about the future. Your symptoms are what you're experiencing, they are not who you are. The good news is that most feelings do eventually pass.

What is the difference between a psychologist and a psychiatrist?

There are several differences between the two, relating to how they train and arrive at this caring profession.

Psychiatrists first train to become a medical doctor and then undertake further training and study to become a psychiatrist.

Psychologists undertake a psychology degree and then complete further practical work and study, sometimes going on to focus on specialised areas.

Psychiatrists prescribe medication, whereas psychologists don't. If you are seeing a psychologist, you'll work in partnership with your referring GP — who *can* prescribe medication if needed. (I needed it!)

What if you don't have money to pay for a psychologist?

There are different ways to access support, depending on where you live, and which country you live in, but there are organisations across the globe that help to connect people who need care with professionals who can help.

You could start by chatting to your doctor about your financial constraints and the possibility of accessing affordable psychology. You could also try getting in touch with your nearest community health centre to see if they have a counsellor or psychologist on staff, asking at your town or city's public hospital about accessing treatment or contacting your local university, as many provide low or no-cost therapy as part of their graduate-training clinics.

In Australia you can get a number of sessions with a Medicare rebate if you are referred via your GP. You may still have to pay between $30 and $50 out of pocket, but honestly it's a small price to pay. (I had very little money when I found myself in this position, and *still* think it was a small price to pay!) There are some bulk-billing psychologists who won't charge you above and beyond the Medicare rebate — so, *zero* out-of-pocket fee — but if you can't find one of these, see if you can save up $12.50 a week and book an appointment once a month. This $50 a month will cover the gap after the Medicare rebate for one session. It might mean forgoing a few cups of coffee or some other little item, but this is important — and sometimes even life-saving — stuff. Don't put it on hold.

That said, mental health care — which really *is* crucial health care — is still not accessible or affordable for many of us, and we need to do much, much better. Let's not skim over that for a second.

But please don't let that get in the way of you committing to spend this money on yourself each month. A mental health care professional can help you recover from terrible times and in the long term, this is money well spent. Take it from me, as someone who suffered unnecessarily for so many years.

If you are not near a psychologist, there are some who practise online. Talkspace and MindSpot are a few online platforms you could take a peek at to get an idea of how this works.

There are also online resources that are helpful. But be warned, there's lots of tough stuff on forums. Things that might upset you, make you feel worse — or even make you worry about the recovery of perfect strangers rather than your own wellbeing. I stay away from forums and Facebook groups for these reasons.

How to find a reputable psychologist

1

Speak to your GP. They will have their own list of reputable clinicians, will create a mental health plan with you (which in Australia makes you eligible to claim a big chunk of the fee through Medicare), and refer you on.

2

Head to the Australian Clinical Psychology Association (ACPA) website. They have a 'find a psychologist' function over there.

Readers outside Australia can find information about finding a therapist through the following bodies:

UK — The British Psychological Society

USA — American Psychological Association

Canada — Canadian Psychological Association

If you're in another part of the world, ask your doctor, or look for the psychological association in your area and use that as a starting point in your search.

What to expect when you head to a psychologist

In different countries, things may roll out a little differently, but here's a general guide about how the sessions may operate.

Standard session times

Your session time will be 50–55 minutes, which leaves a little bit of time for your therapist to write up your notes at the end of your time together. This might seem like a long session at first, but the time will fly by as your person engages you in chatter about what has been going on with you.

Therapeutic stages

These 'stages' are simply a guide, and you may find you go through these more than once depending on how you are feeling.

Assessment — Where you and your therapist get acquainted and discuss why you are there.

Early interventions — Where you and your therapist work on the most pressing issues and begin a treatment plan.

Deepening — If you are seeing your therapist for medium or long-term treatment, this is where you will dig a little deeper and look at more established behavioural patterns and responses, and how these might be impacting your life.

Termination — When you stop having sessions with your therapist, once the therapy goals have been achieved.

Listen carefully
and implement
the strategies you
discuss as much
as possible.

How to be a good therapy subject

I guess for me, the realisation that mental health care is as important as physical health care (and for people in crisis often *even more* important) made going to my sessions non-negotiable. I was a bit frightened of where life was taking me, so my sessions felt like a lifeline. Getting the right support made me feel strong enough to push on, took the edge off my suffering and slowly provided much-needed hope for the future.

Here are a few things you can do to get the most out of your sessions.

Prioritise your therapy

That means not flaking on appointments, being on time and fronting up ready to actively participate in the process.

Be motivated

Listen carefully and implement the strategies you discuss as much as possible. Even if some things might seem like they won't work, give them a whirl and trust your therapist's professional expertise.

Look after your overall health

As you know if you've read this far in this book, physical health impacts on mental health. So making an effort to look after your physical health can only assist the therapy process.

Provide feedback

Let your therapist know what is working for you, and what might not be as effective, so they can tailor your treatment to better suit you.

And take it from me, just having someone to talk to — someone who wants to *be* there and is not fed up with hearing about your struggles — is brilliant and worth every penny.

Friends and family can get a bit worn out or traumatised when they are acting as your therapist, so calling in the professionals can help to free up your friends and family members for some less taxing but equally loving support.

CHAPTER 11

Helpful
new habits

> Creating a new
> life is a like
> putting on a
> new pair of
> shoes: they fit,
> but they feel
> weird.

SOMETIMES THEY HURT, and other times they feel just dandy.

When I was a teenager and things felt tough, I would go into my room, shut the door and move the furniture around. This was no mean feat, because I shared a room with my sister and we had twin desks and bunk beds, and a fish tank. The wall above and around my bunk was plastered with pages torn from magazines — pop stars, fashion, poems, advertising; the whole wall a collage.

I'd get in there, all alone, and begin moving the entire room around. Dragging the bunks across the floor. Remaking the beds to suit their new orientation. Shifting the fish tank, being careful not to slosh the fish out. Plugging in the pump and filter. Moving my record player. Pushing the desks into new spots and tucking chairs underneath them. Pulling down the collage, being careful not to tear the pages, and sticking the pages back up, on another wall, in another way.

When it was all done, it would be neat and new and different. My sister would wander in beaming, as excited as I was about the big change.

I honestly did this every few months for many of my teenage years, and in a weird way it got me through some lonely and worried times. I think there was something about taking control, having my own space and creating a different perspective that gave me a little optimism boost and showed me that most things are temporary. That a bit of a shift can make things feel a little better.

Bend, break and blend

And perhaps, in my teenage years, there was also an element of creativity to this need to keep changing my shared bedroom around?

As neuroscientist Professor David Eagleman says, our brains are driven to 'bend, break and blend'. And in a 2018 essay referencing several brilliant studies, titled 'How craft is good for our health', Professor Susan Luckman wrote about the unique benefits of craft as part of a treatment plan for depression, anxiety and eating disorders.

I don't want to toot my own horn here, but as an author of five books about creativity, and the leader of a craft group called Brown Owls, I can vouch for the benefits of creativity out in the wild.

So if we riff off Dave's work, Susan's research and my own grassroots experience — if we bend, break and blend all these together — it follows that we are built to create, and creating can make us feel better and connect us to others. This is especially important when we're suffering and/or feeling isolated.

Bending, breaking and blending show us that life is not hopeless, that most things are temporary, and that we can use the very same circumstances to do things differently and unexpectedly.

So making time to do new things with our hands, heads and hearts is a way to walk the talk of recovering and move into a different kind of life. And if you're thinking at this point that your creative stripes might not be up to scratch, please think again.

David says that this 'bend, break and blend' cognitive software is loaded into *everybody's* brains, and that this is how human brains work generally. The human brain always wants things that are novel, yet at the same time somehow familiar, tying in to what it already understands.

I guess it's a little like teenage me in my bedroom, taking the same things, dragging them around, putting them together in new ways and coming out of it feeling much better.

Of course, my creativity takes other forms now, but the inbuilt push for this bending, breaking and blending remains.

And I am sure it does in you, too.

Think of this period of recovery as a prime time for flexing those creative muscles even more as you slowly go about resetting yourself.

When you can find little ways to change things up, it's a powerful reminder that new things are possible.

Start a quest

Many people also do some pretty interesting *big* things in their quest to push through those searching, yearning restless times.

After the unexpected death of her father, for example, *H is for Hawk* author Helen Macdonald set to work training a grumpy goshawk as she attempted to find her feet in a world forever shifted.

Grieving the loss of a child, *The Fish Ladder* author Katharine Norbury began walking through the English countryside, tracking a series of rivers from the sea to their source.

Wild author, Cheryl Strayed, dealing with her grief by walking 1100 miles alone along the Pacific Crest Trail as she processed her mother's death.

When *The Outrun* author, Amy Liptrot, reclaimed her sobriety, she returned to her childhood home on an Orkney island to patch herself up and restart her life, and clinging to the idea of writing that very book was what pulled her through.

Jessica J. Lee, author of *Turning: A Swimming Memoir*, swam the lakes surrounding Berlin, hoping to submerge herself in 52 of them over a year as she emerged from depression — despite being terrified of swimming, especially in lakes. She later reflected that it was a way of learning to accept and live with fear.

In the wake of her husband's death, and daughter's severe illness, Joan Didion wrote *The Year of Magical Thinking* 'to bring death up close', finishing it in only 88 days.

I guess these are all restless quests. Challenges undertaken when life has shifted so dramatically that the usual things make little sense.

For some, it can be a powerful way of processing and finally moving forward.

Starting on
a quest can be a
powerful way of
processing and
finally moving
forward.

♥

Adopt a 'progress practice'

Perhaps you are feeling like you're in your own version of *Groundhog Day*, where the days are rolling through, but you don't seem to be feeling any better or adapting very well to your now-different life?

This is where engaging in a 'progress practice' can really help.

Reading, making things, gardening, cooking, organising or writing are all excellent 'progress' practices, where we can see the fruits of our efforts in tangible form. Engaging in such activities can help give a sense of tangible progression when we're otherwise feeling pretty stuck.

Progress practices will be different for everyone, but creative activities in particular are brilliant for helping us push on and find our feet again.

A 2016 study by Otago University found that activities like knitting, crocheting, painting, songwriting and other design-based skills improved the wellbeing of those who practised them. They also found that being creative one day resulted in a sort of positive flow-on into the following day — that creative activity predicted wellbeing the next day.

In other words, regular creativity can help promote positive psychological functioning.

My experiences of losing important people, dealing with challenging physical and mental health issues and trying to navigate heartbreak and trauma have taught me that doing simple things that show progress can provide something solid to cling on to.

Seeing small but positive changes happening outside ourselves can be incredibly heartening and reassuring when things are hard.

Mindfulness

Mindfulness is simply about returning to the present moment.
To pay attention.

In his great book *Mindfulness for Prolonged Grief*, psychologist Sameet
M. Kumar talks about how the mind responds to loss, interpreting
ancient Buddhist practices for a modern world. Indeed, Sameet notes
that mindfulness meditation has helped his own patients deal with a
variety of emotional conditions, and explains that the Buddha himself
encouraged those who were suffering to try mindfulness as a salve.

While we all experience loss and trauma in different ways, the way
our minds respond to these sorts of hardships usually has something
in common.

Kumar says we crave control and permanence when things have
gone awry, and our mind is not particularly discerning about where
that permanence comes from. Indeed, sometimes our *suffering* becomes
the thing that feels permanent.

Our mind is seeking something stable because it doesn't want to
adapt too much or deal with change. Thus, these feelings of pain —
which have become so much the norm — seem a 'stable' place to land
at this point.

This doesn't seem super-helpful of our mind, right? But perhaps
it will help you to know that it's a sort of default response and not some
kind of failing or masochistic bent. Phew. Glad we cleared that up.

Kumar also notes that after loss or trauma, we are often left with a
void where our old life or person was. Faced with this empty space, our
mind tries to fill it up — and that filler is often made up of thoughts
about what we've just endured, playing over and over in an attempt to
reconcile events, and determine where to next.

This is where Kumar points out that mindfulness exercises can be of immense help: by teaching us to redirect and reframe those thoughts, and relieve some of that painful chatter.

Some everyday mindfulness techniques

Hard times are often described with reference to the natural world. People talk about being in a hurricane, weathering a storm, drowning, being in a fog.

Mindfulness is a strategy designed to help find calm in this sort of swirling and out-of-control world. A bit of peace in the eye of a cyclone, if you will.

Here are some simple techniques that can help you get there, if just for a short time.

TWO-MINUTE CHECK-IN

Take a few minutes to stop and ask yourself how you are feeling right this minute. Notice if you are breathing deep or shallow. Fast or slow. Notice if any parts of your body are feeling uncomfortable or in pain. Are you hot or cold? What can you feel or hear or smell?

MINDFUL TIDYING

Do the dishes or fold the laundry, really paying attention to what you're doing. Notice how things look, feel, smell and sound. Take plenty of time to do your task, and do it well. Try to breathe slowly and deeply, and allow yourself to get totally immersed in your work.

MINDFUL COOKING

Slow things right down and pay attention to each part of the process. Maybe it's chopping your vegetables carefully, listening to the sizzle of butter as it melts, smelling the fragrant garlic as it fries, tumbling the ingredients into the pan. Really notice what is going on instead of trying to get a step ahead of the process.

A FEEL-GOOD STRETCH

Lie on the floor. Breathe slowly and deeply from your belly. Slowly stretch your arms, then legs, then neck, then back. Stretch in a way that feels good to you. Really notice how each part of your body feels as you do this. Are there any clues that can help you feel a little better today? Maybe you need to take regular breaks from work or do a more targeted five-minute yoga session? (Head to YouTube for hundreds of those.) Keep breathing as you stretch.

WRITE A LIST OF GOOD THINGS

Not only can writing a list of good things help you find the highlights in a day that might have seemed lacklustre, it can also reframe the days ahead in a more positive way, making you much more aware of the good things around you. Noticing the puppy that let you scratch his belly today will mean you're much more likely to notice the belly-offering puppies that cross your path tomorrow.

Mindfulness is a whopping topic, to be honest. I am only a beginner-level mindfulness practitioner so I would recommend you tap into some more definitive guides to this practice if it's something you feel will help you. (And I think it will help you!) You could start with Sameet M. Kumar's book *Mindfulness for Prolonged Grief* or Ruby Wax's *A Mindfulness Guide for the Frazzled*.

Live the homebody life

Sometimes a loss or personal crisis makes us forget what it feels like to be us. It can be helpful to start thinking about the things that help you feel like yourself, and even to remember some of the things you loved to do in 'pre-crap times'.

As I kid I knew instinctively that there are comforts of home that have the power to make you feel like you truly belong, and that the world is an excellent place. A lot of these intersect with mindfulness.

FOR ME, SOME OF THESE HOME COMFORTS FROM MY EARLY DAYS INCLUDE:

- Eating a perfectly bubbly, golden slice of cheese on toast in a giant armchair, as the radio drones in the background.

- Clinking ice into long glasses and slugging blackcurrant cordial across their frosty cubes, creaking the tap on to fill them and seal the sweet, tinkly deal.

- Smoothing blankets across fresh linen sheets before sliding my sandy feet underneath, and pulling a book and the sheets up to my chin.

- Sitting at the kitchen table, opening a new notebook and brushing my fingers across the page as I bring pencil to paper for the very first, new-book-smelling time.

- Waking up before everyone else and setting a fire, then lighting it and feeding it little twigs from the garden until it was roaring, then slowing to a cosy, steady crackle and snap.

These homey rituals are simple, but they mark the kind of tiny, perfect moments that make me feel perfectly capable of being just me.

As an adult I remain ridiculously focused on the homebody life, and the comfort and rituals that come into play at home.

Our home is a retreat from the world. A place where we feel so much like us that we don't ever have to adjust ourselves to fit. A place where we can breathe, relax and belong. Ideally, it should be filled with the sort of books, films, music, art, textiles, colours and *things* that make us feel good.

Pay attention to the homey circumstances that create a tiny spark in you. Which bits of home make you feel a little restored?

For me, it's things like making a perfectly delicious cup of coffee, working in front of big bright windows, having lovely green plants and fresh flowers around the place, shelves stocked with zillions of books, the sound of birds, cosy soft furnishings to feather my nest, nice music or the drone of the radio, colourful art on the walls, fragrant candles, a laptop loaded with good things to watch, a pot of soup on the stove, the promise of good snacks in the pantry ...

Maybe some of these are on your helpful home habits list, too?

A home reminds of how to be ourselves, which is especially useful when we're not feeling great, or might have even forgotten who we are.

'Wherever you are, at any moment, try and find something beautiful. A face, a line out of a poem, the clouds out of a window, some graffiti, a wind farm. Beauty cleans the mind.' — Matt Haig, *Reasons to Stay Alive*

Finding new ways to think and feel

I thought it might also be a good idea to talk about some other therapeutic ways that might help you feel better.

You can look into them yourself and/or chat to a therapist about them.

Promoting unconditional positive regard

Unconditional positive regard is an attitude of love and acceptance for yourself or for another person. It means accepting and caring for yourself or others on a deep level, with kindness and without judgement.

Creating a WRAP

Dr Mary Ellen Copeland authored the original WRAP, or Wellness Recovery Action Plan. A WRAP can arm us with tools that help us stay well, spark helpful daily habits, spot stressors and respond to them in a more informed way.

Trying compassion-focused therapy

Compassion-focused therapy (CFT) promotes healing by encouraging self-compassion and compassion towards others. It might involve mindfulness exercises, learning to reframe thoughts and situations so that the body's soothing system is activated, learning to focus more closely on positive experiences — and a bunch of other stuff a trained professional can help you explore.

Trying cognitive behavioural therapy

I'm sure you've heard of cognitive behavioural therapy (CBT), as it is very widely used. CBT aims to identify unhelpful thoughts and challenge them with a more helpful and healthy response. There are heaps of books on the subject, or you can work on this with a professional.

Practising loving kindness meditation

Another compassion-themed approach, this is also known as 'metta meditation'. The idea here is that the more we bring loving kindness into our life — and meditate on it — the more we nurture compassion, reconcile suffering and let go of judgement. Definitely worth a try.

Get bendy

For a brain and body helper, I'd also highly recommend doing some yoga at home in some comfy old clothes. I stretch along to 'Yoga With Adriene'. You can find her via her website of the same name or free YouTube videos. (Thank you, Adriene!)

I love doing yoga at home because you can do it at any time and feel the benefits.

'A little goes a long way', as Adriene says.

CHAPTER 12

A life
transformed

*The glory of the day
was in her face,*

*The beauty of the
night was in her eyes.*

*And over all her
loveliness, the grace
Of Morning blushing
in the early skies.*

James Weldon
Johnson, from
his poem
'The Glory of
the Day Was in
Her Face'

YOU WILL NOT always feel utterly terrible. You will, some day in your own good time, feel different to that, and begin to realise that things are slowly shifting.

That's not to say we completely get over difficult experiences, but we do learn how to absorb them into our lives, eventually. Each in our own way.

Weirdly, sometimes it feels a bit scary to let that 'soaking in' happen. We're used to holding our breath, being on edge and keeping our suffering close.

Perhaps you might need a little reminder to stop holding your breath or expecting more of the worst?

Consider yourself reminded, when the time is right. Maybe it's in a month or maybe it's in a year or maybe it'll take longer than that.

Just keep an eye out for those quiet or happy or unexpected moments where you start to feel more hopeful and a bit more like your (new) self. Somehow noticing those positive mini-shifts encourages more of the same.

I don't feel like that anymore

One afternoon my son Ari was ruffling about in the freezer and said he'd bought some ice cream and I should have some if I felt like it.

'Aw thanks,' I told him. 'I'm not really eating ice cream anymore. Not like I used to.'

Ari said, 'Gawd, remember when you used to just have ice cream for dinner sometimes?'

'I know!' I said, 'It was like my hospital food ... when I was too sad to make anything I'd just have ice cream!'

I stopped, and added: 'I don't feel like that anymore.'

And then Ari shut the freezer and gave me a big hug. It was my first ever post-freezer-squiz hug ... and it meant a lot to me.

Another time I started to feel better, having had two *quite okay* days in a row. I took to social media to tell everyone *I was feeling better*! Then I went for a late-night walk to meet Ari on his way home and fell over a bit of wood. And smashed my face. And my knee. And spent the next week with a sore jaw and various aches and pains.

The moral of this story is that it can be swings and roundabouts; a week later I was feeling *okay* again.

Difficulty can be a sort of rebirth, an unwanted one, granted. Your life is different, you are different, the way your body and brain feel are different.

Sometimes different ideas begin to flow. Now you might be thinking, '*Eff* ideas! I just want things to be less crap!' Honestly, I hear you. But maybe this focus shift, this complete rearrangement of how the world feels, might hold some glimmers of opportunity and surprise amidst the tough stuff.

Perhaps, as wounds begin to feel less raw, you can look for those glimmers and think about what they mean and whether they might mark a new direction you could wander off in from time to time, away from the worst bits of right now.

Maybe these new glimmers can distract you, at least for a moment, from the adjustments you are going through?

In 2017, two years after the death of his son Earl, singer–songwriter Nick Cave spoke to *The Guardian* about loss, life and work, and reflected on how things felt and shifted: 'Like there's just this thing, and there's no way to navigate it. It just sits there and it fills up all the space. It fills up your body. It's like a physical thing. You can feel it pressing against the insides of your fingers. There's just no room for the luxury of creation.' He continued: 'I don't feel like that anymore, I have to say ... I feel I have turned a corner and wandered on to a landscape that is open and vast.'

One thing that can be really hard to stop obsessing over is whether things could have been another way.

'Everyone has a sliding door moment,' says Turia Pitt, a brilliant woman who was severely injured when a wildfire crossed the path of an ultramarathon in which she was running. 'What if you took that job opportunity? What if you didn't move? What if you and such and such didn't break up? What if you had kids with your first boyfriend? You can spend a lot of time going down that rabbit hole,' she adds, 'but it's kind of pointless because it doesn't achieve anything. I don't really think about what my life would have been like because this is my life now.'

I've spoken to my psychologist a little about this ... about what power we might have over some of the things that happen in life. Granted, we do sometimes have some power over events, but other times it's actually a series of sequential decisions that steers us in one direction or another — a bunch of micro-moves that get us to where we end up.

'I do remember the pain. What you really forget is love.'

So, if we had our time over again and wanted things to turn out differently, it would very often be a lot of little shifts we'd have to make, rather than one big 'sliding doors' moment.

This is good news because if you are constantly blaming yourself for where you find yourself — and let's face it, lots of us do — you would've had to make a giant and epic consistent effort to change so many things, for things to have landed differently.

You. Did. The. Best. You. Could. Do. At. The. Time.

Author Nora Ephron famously penned the book *Heartburn* about the end of her marriage. 'My religion is Get Over It,' she wrote in *I Remember Nothing: and other reflections*. 'I turned it into a rollicking story. I wrote a novel and bought a house with the money from it. People always say you forget the pain. It's a cliché of childbirth, too. I don't happen to agree. I do remember the pain. What you really forget is love.'

The remarkable Maya Angelou lived through early childhood sexual trauma that left her unable to speak, she endured racism, suffered heartbreak over and over, and came out of it ... transformed.

You. Did.
The. Best.
You. Could.
Do. At.
The. Time.

♥

'I can be changed by what happens to me. But I refuse to be reduced by it,' Maya Angelou famously said. And she certainly wasn't reduced by it; instead she became a powerful civil rights activist, a prolific writer of books, poems and screenplays, a winner of scores of humanitarian and literary awards — and the recipient of more than 50 honorary degrees.

The losses or difficulties we endure not only change us, they remain with us. They become part of us.

In her book *M Train*, singer–songwriter Patti Smith spoke about the death of her brother Todd so soon after her husband Fred died. She was crossing the street when she realised she was crying. 'Who is in my heart?' she asked herself. She thought about her brother and the positivity that defined much of his life. 'As I continued my walk I slowly reclaimed an aspect of him that was also myself — a natural optimism.'

Even the most acutely painful events somehow find their natural place as the days roll on.

Singer Lily Allen's baby boy George died just six months into her pregnancy. Describing how she kept going after such an incredibly traumatic and life-altering event, Lily said that George is central to the life she was somehow able to piece back together.

'Your lost child is there with you. Always. This beautiful, negative space inside you forever," she wrote in *My Thoughts Exactly*.

Sometimes you think you know what the ending will be ... and it turns out completely differently, because life is somehow always keen to surprise us — and when you're living so deeply in the minutes and hours you've been enduring, it's very hard to think ahead with any clarity.

When singer Edwyn Collins suffered several life-threatening brain haemorrhages in 2005, his wife Grace Maxwell wrote of the family's experiences as he recovered. 'When this first happened to Edwyn, we all did our best not to get engulfed by the hugeness of it all,' Grace told *The Independent* newspaper in 2009.

'We just tried to work through it,' she said, 'and keep ourselves busy. That was the important thing. I had lots of fantasies, especially about Edwyn being able to get back up on stage, but I never for a moment imagined it would ever come to pass. The fact that it now has is something I can barely absorb. It is truly amazing, and I am so proud of him, so happy.'

Former model and TV presenter Katie Piper was raped and the target of an acid attack. She's spent the last decade recovering and transforming her life, creating the podcast 'Katie Piper's Extraordinary People' to tell the stories of other brilliant humans who have tackled adversity.

'We can choose the attitude we take to every day,' Katie told the website Lumity. 'While we can't change the past or other people, we can change what we do … we can be generous and we can help others.'

Maya Angelou agrees. 'My wish for you is that you continue. Continue to be who and how you are, to astonish a mean world with your acts of kindness. Continue to allow humour to lighten the burden of your tender heart.'

Even the most acutely painful events somehow find their natural place as the days roll on.

Promoting resilience

So what helps to foster this kind of recovery and resilience, apart from the passing of time? From my own research into the topic and personal experience, here are 10 themes that pop up time and time again.

1. Have an optimistic nature.

2. Nurture your ability to reframe negative thoughts or situations by looking for meaning, benefits, or that oft-talked of 'silver lining'.

3. Know that it's okay to use humour to cope with hard times.

4. Use active coping strategies to deal with stress, rather than avoidant ones. Active coping refers to taking action or making an effort to remove or circumvent stressors; avoidant coping would be behaviours such as misusing alcohol and drugs.

5. Tap into or seek support from others.

6. Take time for physical activity, and avoid being sedentary if you can.

7. Practise pro-social or altruistic behaviour — think about doing things for others and being as kind as you can.

8. Practise mindfulness often.

9. Tap into any spiritual and/ or moral beliefs.

10. Check in with yourself each day, making a daily self-care plan based on how you are feeling.

A different world

There are lots of ways to look after yourself as you live through difficult days, but it's also important to remember that you're getting to know a different you.

The ideas in this book can help you push on when you don't recognise yourself or your circumstances. And with the passing of time, this strange new world and different sort of you will begin to feel more familiar.

Perhaps it's not a particularly shiny sort of you just yet, but honestly, nobody is totally shiny all of the time, and nor is life generally.

In fact, who even says shiny is the ideal? Maybe gently opaque is your thing? Brilliant. Perhaps you're occasionally luminous? Ace. You might even be fascinatingly dusky or just a tiny bit twinkly (but mostly on a Friday night).

The world needs those types of humans, too.

And look, we might not be the shiny ones right this minute — but we can work at being the ones who are keen to learn, the ones who try hard to listen, the ones who share compassion. For others and for ourselves.

So go do that, you occasionally luminous/gently opaque/tiny bit twinkly GEM!

End bits

Pip's fortifying playlist

(Curated by my buddy writer, DJ and broadcaster Steve Wide)

Hug My Soul Saint Etienne

Shout To The Top Style Council

Life's What You Make It Talk Talk

Walking On Sunshine Katrina & the Waves

Lust For Life Iggy Pop

Ain't No Mountain High Enough Marvin Gaye and Tammi Terrell

Happy Song Boney M.

Born To Be Alive Patrick Hernandez

Don't Stop Me Now Queen

Feeling Good Nina Simone

Heroes David Bowie

Feel Good Inc. Gorillaz

Dancing In The Moonlight Toploader

Alright Supergrass

Positivity/Everything Will Flow Suede

Shout Lulu

Good Vibrations The Beach Boys

I've Been To A Marvellous Party Noël Coward/The Divine Comedy

Friday I'm In Love The Cure

Stronger Kanye West

NeverEnding Story Limahl

Fanfare for the Common Man Emerson, Lake & Palmer

Just Can't Get Enough Depeche Mode

Bring The Noise Public Enemy

Pure Lightning Seeds

Brilliant Trees David Sylvian

Such Great Heights Postal Service

Mis-Shapes Pulp

Golden Hair Slowdive

Surfing On A Rocket Air

We Own The Sky M83

Soleil Françoise Hardy

Such a Remarkable Day Charlotte Gainsbourg

Island In The Sun Weezer

Zou Bisou Bisou Cover by Jessica Paré (Megan) in *Mad Men*

Bridge Over Troubled Water Simon and Garfunkel

Rocket Man Cover by Peyton Kennedy (Kate) in *Everything Sucks*

Strength in Numbers The Music

Perfect Day Lou Reed

Tubthumping Chumbawamba

Some informative, inspiring reads for the beleaguered

SCIENCE-Y AND/OR CALMING

Shame: free yourself, find joy, and build true self-esteem by Joseph Burgo

The Pocket Pema Chödrön by Pema Chödrön

When Things Fall Apart by Pema Chödrön

Mindfulness for Prolonged Grief by Sameet M. Kumar

Brain Changer: The Good Mental Health Diet by Professor Felice Jacka

Blue Mind by Wallace J. Nichols

Learned Optimism by Martin Seligman

Can You Die of a Broken Heart? by Dr Nikki Stamp

Love for Imperfect Things by Haemin Sunim

Why We Sleep by Matthew Walker

A Mindfulness Guide for the Frazzled by Ruby Wax

The Nature Fix by Florence Williams

MEMOIRS

My Thoughts Exactly by Lily Allen

We'll Always Have Paris by Emma Beddington

The Stranger on the Bridge by Jonny Benjamin

We Took to The Woods by Louise Dickinson

The Year of Magical Thinking by Joan Didion

Heartburn by Nora Ephron

Reasons to Stay Alive by Matt Haig

Lab Girl by Hope Jahren

Rachel's Holiday by Marian Keyes

Saved by Cake by Marian Keyes

Turning: A swimming memoir by Jessica J. Lee

Craft for the Soul by Pip Lincolne

The Outrun by Amy Liptrot

H is for Hawk by Helen Macdonald

Falling and Laughing: The restoration of Edwyn Collins by Grace Maxwell

The Fish Ladder by Katharine Norbury

Encyclopedia of an Ordinary Life by Amy Krouse Rosenthal

The May Beetles by Baba Schwartz

Wild by Cheryl Strayed

Educated by Tara Westover

The Sheep Stell by Janet White

SPECIAL MENTION

One More Time With Feeling — the Nick Cave Documentary

RESOURCES

beyondblue.org.au

blackdoginstitute.org.au

headstogether.org.uk

phoenixaustralia.org

5 ways to feel better when things have gone wrong

1. Have a pity party

We *all* know that alcohol is a depressant, and that 'alcohol is not the answer'. But sometimes having a few Pimms or pints or gin and tonics with your buddies and sobbing into a beer coaster is just the kind of companionship you need. Note that the pity party is really a one-night-only offering. Having a pity party (or a solo pity party) every night really isn't advisable or helpful.

2. Pat an animal

Hanging out with animals can help us feel more grounded. If you have a pet, you are well on your way to some small doses of 'feeling better'. Animals are a reminder that there are big, amazing, complex systems at play out there in the natural world. This makes us feel a bit less *big* and a bit more like we are part of something *bigger*. If you don't have a pet, getting out amongst nature can be a good alternative. Speaking of which ...

3. Walk it out

Being out in the world amongst the trees and the chirpy birds and the snails and the ants is a calming tonic if you're feeling overwhelmed. Avoid maudlin meandering. If you walk for long enough or at a decent pace, your endorphins will reward you, but even a little bit of fresh air and fresh perspective can clear the head and help you find your feet.

4. Write it all down

This is my favourite thing, as you may have noticed! Write down all the things that are worrying you. It's not a novel or fancy prose; it's for your eyes only. Think about the feelings that are washing over you. How it feels. Why you feel that way. What happened. Who was there. Write, write, write. Then come back later and do it again. Do this every day. Get it all out.

5. Treat yourself

I'm not talking about racking up totally bonkers charges on your credit card, but maybe it's time to take yourself out for a little treat, and indulge just a little in the kind of things that make you feel sparklier? For me that might involve books, op shop ceramics, vintage dresses, kimchi, nice stationery, white chocolate, bunches of fragrant flowers, colourful socks, nice perfume, new leggings (*I know!*) ... Don't spend too much, but why not shout yourself a few little pick-me-ups.

10 ways to feel bright as a button

1. Get in touch with three friends. Yes, three. Text someone out of the blue. Write a card and pop it in the post. Drop a care package on a pal's doorstep. There's nothing like your friends to help you find your place in the world and remind you how good your life really is.

2. Write an important letter. Even though the internet *loves* a petition, why not be even more proactive and put pen to paper to protest a wrong or support a cause you love? Not only are you tapping into the meaningful stuff that makes you tick, you might even impact on someone else's life in a positive way.

3. Go bird spotting. So often we head out to get our 'steps' up or to burn calories or just to tick the 'exercise' thing off our daily (weekly?!) list. Don't forget how great it is to have an amble with *no* real purpose except to notice cool stuff that's not only nature-y, but capable of reminding us that there's heaps of wonder in the world. Yay!

4. Dance around the kitchen to a tune that brings a little nostalgic delight.

5. Eat some bread. Or some cake. Or some ice cream. Just eat something you love and don't even tell me that you can't do that because they're carbs or 'sometimes foods' or any of that piffle. Food is for fun too, remember?! Eat it with pleasure, and thank your body for being just the way it is.

6. Look at a picture of a sloth.

7. Do some drawing or colouring in. You don't have to show it to anyone. Speak with a pompous accent to yourself about how interesting and unexpected your work is. Do that.

8. Float around in some water.

9. Sing very loudly to quite bad music. This is self-explanatory, but you should know that a) censoring yourself and b) avoiding undignified dance moves are definitely *out*. Sing from your diaphragm. Dance with your shoulders. The world is your stage.

10. Pick something. Some flowers, herbs, fruit. (If you get caught picking someone else's stuff, do not blame me. Nuh-uh.)

5 ace gems to look for in your life

1. The things you have achieved that you have sort of forgotten about

I think this is such a modern-life thing! We're encouraged to be goal-focused and not rest on our laurels, but it stops us from taking the time to think about how far we've come and the things we might have achieved. Get a pen and paper, write down the good things you've done so far. Keep adding to the list and give yourself a blinking good pat on the back for doing your best.

2. The smell of something good — perfume, brewing coffee, frying garlic, flowers on the way to the bus stop

Rushing from A to B is really not a cool idea. Go from A to BE instead and find sensory ways to connect with the world around you. Slow down and smell the roses. Yes. Actually really *do* that. A great way to ground yourself a little, and confirm your steady place in the chaos, is to focus your senses on the good stuff around you. It's a bit like looking for the light, except instead of using your eyes, you use your nose! I know! Genius! Be thankful for wild freesias, baking bread, simmering soup, the neighbour's freshly mown lawn. Use these fragrant gems to mark nice moments in your day, so you can stop and think about what's going great for you, right there and then.

3. The beautiful light in your room/house/world/life

In a world full of stuff, there are many special things (like rainbows, nice breezes and dew drops) that cannot be owned. The pretty light that crops up as you go about your day is one of those special things. Make a sometimes ritual of noticing when the light is doing its special snazzy thing near you. Mumble a nice compliment to the universe and soak it up for as long as you can. Noticing you're part of something beautiful that's way bigger than you is such a calming, positive ritual.

4. The people who love you for you, no matter how long it's been since you saw them

Think about how *great* some of your fave people are and what they bring to your life. Imagine what you'd say about your friendships if someone was filming you for a documentary about friendships. (Well you *never know!*) Count your friendly blessings, is what I am saying here.

5. The sneaky chortle, when something delightful catches you by surprise

We like to think we can mostly keep a lid on our emotions, but the sneaky chortle begs to differ. It wants you to know that you're ever-changing, that life is full of possibilities and joy is always an option, sometimes when you least expect it. Add some funny books to your reading list. Watch a few comedies that were made in the '80s and '90s, before everyone got super0polished and scripts were workshopped within an inch of their life. (Snorts are gems too, btw!)

20 quick things to do
when you are feeling slumpy

1. Have a rest, with a blanket and pillow and the like.

2. Take a bath! Some like it hot, some like it bubbly.

3. Take a gentle walk.

4. Write it down. Just take pen to paper or put fingers to keyboard and go nuts. It doesn't have to make sense.

5. Make a delicious snack. Soup? Cake? Roast potatoes?

6. Watch something funny.

7. Watch something sad and get it all out.

8. Clear your schedule. You deserve a break to help the slump pass.

9. Read a book.

10. Buy a rocking chair. (I did this today and it cheered me up no end. It might work for you, too!)

11. Smell something nice — perfume that reminds you of your mum, fresh flowers, lavender … it will calm you.

12. Meditate. I am bad at this, but even I can do it if I use the Smiling Mind app.

13. Do some gentle stretches.

14. Cook something from your childhood.

15. Find a big view to look at. Honestly, it really helps. Your slump will seem less huge when you look at something marvellous and big.

16. Phone a friend. Ring someone up for a chat. It's nice to do that instead of messaging online.

17. Do something nice for someone else. Send a thank you card, fan email or care package.

18. Gather *yourself* a care package: go to the shops and buy some special treats just for *you*.

19. Start a small project (such as something crafty or in the garden) where you see tangible progress.

20. Find a nice pal or pet to hug or pat.

Thank you

To Rin, Max, Ari and Paul. And Mum, Nan, Sara, Andy and Sean.

To Jane Morrow and Pippa Masson for believing this book was worth publishing.

To the professionals who helped me: Dr Christina Bryant, Dr Jeanne Knapp.

To the team at Murdoch Books for their care and kindness as we made this book together.

To Yvonne for being the best buddy during the worst times.

To Kirsty, Victoria and Gemma.

To Kerry Athanasiadis, Michelle Mackintosh, Steve Wide, Gill Stannard for their contributions to this book.

To my friends and work buddies who egged me on.

To my brilliant and so loyal and very funny blog readers and internet buddies.

To everyone who sent me a message during my hard times.

To the other writers who got me through.

To Nick Cave for the soundtrack.

To Bean, Mike and Peach for the pats and love.

INDEX

Published in 2020 by Murdoch Books,
an imprint of Allen & Unwin

Murdoch Books Australia
83 Alexander Street
Crows Nest NSW 2065
Phone: +61 (0)2 8425 0100
murdochbooks.com.au
info@murdochbooks.com.au

Murdoch Books UK
Ormond House, 26–27 Boswell Street,
London, WC1N 3JZ
Phone: +44 (0) 20 8785 5995
murdochbooks.co.uk
info@murdochbooks.co.uk

For corporate orders & custom publishing, contact our
business development team at salesenquiries@murdochbooks.com.au.

Publisher: Jane Morrow
Designer: Michelle Mackintosh
Creative Manager: Vivien Valk
Editor: Katri Hilden
Proofreader: Katie Bosher
Editorial Manager: Justin Wolfers
Production Director: Lou Playfair

ISBN 9 781 76052 479 1 Australia
ISBN 9 781 91163 237 5 UK

A cataloguing-in-publication entry is
available from the catalogue of the
National Library of Australia at nla.gov.au.

A catalogue record for this book is available from the British Library

Colour reproduction by Splitting Image Colour Studio Pty Ltd, Clayton, Victoria
Printed by C & C Offset Printing Co Ltd, China

MIX
Paper from
responsible sources
FSC
www.fsc.org   FSC® C008047

The paper in this book is FSC® certified. FSC®
promotes environmentally responsible, socially
beneficial and economically viable management
of the world's forests.